The
Management of
Remuneration

paying for effectiveness

Ian Smith

The Institute of Personnel Management and Gower

For my son Peter

© *Institute of Personnel Management 1983*
First published 1983

Paperback edition published by the Institute of Personnel Management, 35 Camp Road, Wimbledon, London SW19 4UV. 1983.

Hardback edition published by Gower Publishing Company Limited, Aldershot, Hants. 1983.

Note: the convention has been followed whereby *he* and *him* are used to cover *she* and *her* wherever appropriate.

British Library Cataloguing in Publication Data

Smith, Ian
 The management of remuneration
 1. Wages
 I. Title
 331.2′15   HD4909

ISBN 0–85292–305–8
ISBN 0–566–02478–0

Printed and bound in Great Britain by
Biddles Ltd, Guildford and King's Lynn

Syed Zahle

Luv's . You All

THE MANAGEMENT OF REMUNERATION
PAYING FOR EFFECTIVENESS

Ian Smith was born and brought up in South-east Lancashire. His first experiences of industry were gained on the shop floor of A V Roe and Co Ltd, Manchester. After graduating from university, he moved to Canada in 1965 and worked in the market forecasting unit of a Montreal chemicals company. In 1966 he joined the Hydro-Electric Power Commission of Ontario in Toronto, first using his economist training in industrial relations and then in industrial engineering. In the latter post he was thoroughly trained in work study and operations/production management.

At the end of 1970 he returned to Britain to specialize on pay and productivity at University College, Cardiff and was awarded an MSc in Economics. He later became Senior Lecturer in Management in the Department of Industrial Relations and Management Studies. In 1979 he was awarded a PhD by the University of Wales for research into national, regional and company level manpower planning.

He is primarily interested in the management of the human resource and the links with production and organization performance. Much of his research work in this area has been presented in many publications including the 'Measurement of Productivity', published by Gower Press and articles on pay, manpower planning and industrial relations in *Industrial Relations Journal*, *Personnel Review*, *Management Today* and *New Society*. He is a member of the British Institute of Management and the Institute of Personnel Management. He has been active in the Cardiff and Newport Branch of the IPM and has served on the National Committee for Manpower Planning.

The engineering industry, and the shop floor environment in particular, have always been of immense interest to Dr Smith. He has provided substantial advisory services to many firms on pay system design, management development and organization design. This work has taken place in chemicals, all types of engineering, textiles, specialist steels and newspaper organizations. He has also provided advice to the Department of Health and Social Security, the Royal Air Force and the Welsh Office on incentive scheme design and management development.

Contents

PART V   CONCLUSION

List of Figures

List of Tables

Acknowledgements

I have always been grateful for the valuable advice and ideas received in discussions with my colleagues in the Department of Industrial Relations and Management Studies at University College, Cardiff, in particular Professor G F Thomason, Peter Anthony and John Bridge. For advice received in the preparation of material for the section on incentive schemes, I should like to record my thanks to J H Clarkson, P Hesketh and D G French. I would also like to thank Sally Harper of the Institute of Personnel Management for her forbearance and helpful co-operation in the preparation of the manuscript. Finally, a thank you to my wife, Carole, for typing the manuscript and preparing diagrams in final form.

Introduction

This book is concerned with wages, salaries and benefits and their effective management. A basic premise of the work is that such effective management should be based on an understanding of structural and behavioural issues (which directly and indirectly influence the provision of pay and benefits) in addition to an evaluation of methods and techniques appropriate to the process of determining pay.

Why remuneration?

The subject of pay in employing organizations is fragmented into what amount to bits and pieces of payments and techniques. Wage and salary administration in much of British industry is a depressingly untidy affair. Any tidying up exercise requires an overall strategy in the first instance, and the theme of this book is provided by a performance orientated strategy for relating managerial decisions on pay to corporate need for well-being or performance. In these terms wages, salaries and benefits might be more appropriately treated as rewards or remunerations rather than compensation. Oxford Dictionary definitions of the words include the following:

Compensation   . . . . . make amends . . . . . for damage . . . . . amount given that serves to . . . .

Remuneration   reward, pay for service rendered . . . . . what is received as pay . . . . .

In texts on personnel management in general, and wages and salaries in particular, the word compensation tends to have preferred usage. But employers are not making amends, or balancing out some form of damage inflicted on their employees, and whatever we may think of our jobs the payment we receive, and the benefits, are not taken as compensation. Therefore, compensation may not be the word to define wages, salaries and benefits adequately and acceptably. Employees give

1

something to the employer, skill, brainpower, time, effort, loyalty, experience and so forth: they are not compensated for that but rewarded. Therefore this book is concerned with the management of remuneration.

Who should read this book?

Because of the complex and fragmentary nature of the subject of remuneration, the book has been divided into four parts plus a concluding chapter. This may allow the reader to choose those subjects that are of particular interest without the need to 'wade' through the rest of the book. It should be noted, however, that the book as a whole is an attempt to provide a comprehensive discussion of the theory and practice, and the current and salient issues in the management of remuneration. Therefore, the book is designed to interest students, particularly those pursuing course requirements for membership of the Institute and those studying for higher degrees in personnel management, managers involved in the practice of wage and salary administration, and executives concerned to understand more of the fundamental issues to be tackled.

Part I: purpose, theory and organization role for the management of remuneration

The cost attached to wages, salaries and benefits is often large enough to influence significantly the financial well-being of the employing organization. Thus management should look for a return from remuneration which is somehow linked into organization performance while meeting the expectations of interested parties. Chapter 1 attempts to clarify this issue and suggests a strategy for the management of remuneration which can be supportive to corporate well-being.

It would be misleading to assume that a purpose for remuneration could be viable without reference to the economic, social and political forces which have been proved to exert some influence on the determination of pay. Therefore, the first part of chapter 2 concentrates on the history of developments in wage theory and assesses the reality and unpredictability of events in the labour market. If remuneration policies and structures are to cope with those unpredictable forces in the labour market, management must develop a clearly defined role for remuneration. The second part of chapter 2 considers this role in the areas of recruitment, retention and motivation, and assesses the contribution of remuneration to the achievement of effectiveness in these areas by attention to the issue of equity in the management of pay.

The main and collective purpose of these two chapters is the identification of the full complexity of issues affecting management decisions about remuneration. These issues are economic, social and political in the main, and can be managed effectively within a purposive approach to the management of pay and benefits which is consistent with corporate requirements for performance.

Part II: structure and design in the management of remuneration

The application of a policy for remuneration involves the determination of pay levels which reflect and support the organization's need to attract and retain effective employees who feel motivated to contribute to the well-being of the company. To realize the advantages of such an approach to managing remuneration requires the rational and methodical design of remuneration structures and the elements of this task are the concern of section 2.

Chapter 3 discusses the characteristics of current structures and the reasons why they have become difficult to manage. It goes on to consider the role of job evaluation in providing a solution. It is the differences in money terms which exist between different jobs and between pay ranges which commonly create problems. To design differentials rationally and in the interests of meeting employee needs for equity remains a complex task.

Chapter 4 examines the characteristics and relative merits of the different methods of job evaluation available to help in the task of designing structures. The elements of procedure and application are also considered.

The actual task of designing rational and manageable remuneration structures is the concern of chapter 5. Job evaluation is discussed in the chapter but is not regarded as essential to the outcome of acceptable structures. The determination of pay is developed step by step with the use of pay surveys, the determination of grades, differentials, overlap, number of pay ranges and span of ranges culminating in a graded structure which can reflect the organization's remuneration policy.

Part III: a consideration of incentives for the management of remuneration

Incentive payments as an element of remuneration represent an important and seemingly immovable part of managerial attempts to

3

influence worker behaviour and company performance in terms of productivity. During the past two decades, many of these schemes have been criticized for failing to improve industrial productivity, causing wage drift and inflation and giving rise to industrial disputes. In answer to this criticism, schemes have been refined and developed and one or two newer approaches to the provision of incentives have appeared. A considerable variety of schemes are therefore available to organizations and making a choice requires care and serious evaluation.

To provide some understanding of schemes and the pitfalls to be avoided, chapter 6 examines the basic principles and objectives of incentive schemes and chapter 7 analyses the main types of scheme available for application. Schemes for manual, white collar and managerial employee groups are considered.

The failure of the vast majority of methods for providing incentives has been a depressing feature of post-war industrial experience in Britain. Chapter 8 attempts to synthesize the basic elements which should make for incentives which adequately and equitably reward employee contributions to performance, impact on company performance and control costs.

Part IV: fringe benefits

Although often devalued by management and workers when considering priorities in remuneration, fringe benefits have become a significant portion of the payroll and the means to improving the security and well-being of all employees considerably. The role of benefits promoting goodwill towards the organization is important and should be recognized by management. In recent years, benefits have been affected by changes in legislation particularly in the areas of pensions, company cars and sick pay, and more management attention to detail is now necessary. Chapter 9 discusses these issues with reference to the main types of benefits against the backcloth of an overall policy for benefits.

Part V: conclusion

A retrospective note on the management of remuneration and a consideration of present and future developments are the concern of chapter 10.

A further note on incentives

A significant proportion of the material contained in Part 3 has been presented to more than 1500 senior executives, from a cross-section of British industry, in seminars held between 1978 and 1982. It has stimulated considerable interest and discussion. There has not been space to provide an in depth appreciation of the work measurement side of incentive design, but I hope sufficient reference has been made to the main issues. Discussion in the section is concentrated on the major problems currently requiring attention by management.

Department of Industrial Relations and Management Studies
University College
Cardiff

May 1983

Part I

A CONSIDERATION
of the purpose theory and
organizational role for the
management of remuneration

1
Purpose and performance

The vast majority of those who read these pages will be receiving some form of income from an employer. Normally such an income will be thought of as a wage or salary which employers provide in return for the availability of time, skill, experience, brainpower and effort which employees bring forward in differing proportions. To a lesser extent, people will consider their income from the employer to embrace fringe benefits such as holidays with pay, pension schemes, company cars and the like. Income, in the form of a wage, may be made up of several payments including overtime, shift differentials, productivity bonus and inconvenience or 'dirt' money. Salaries may also contain more than one component, for example, a merit payment. The wage has traditionally been regarded as the word to describe the hourly based and weekly paid income of a manual or blue collar worker. The salary has traditionally been considered the word to describe the monthly income of white collar administrative and managerial workers. Wages are normally paid in cash. Salaries are normally paid directly into the employee's bank account. A degree of mystique and status has long surrounded the 'salary', not so strong now, but the salary is still regarded in many companies almost as a type of perquisite, ie to say you are salaried is to suggest receiving something rather more than just a payment. During the 1960s and 1970s, many companies conferred salary status on manual employees as if this alone, with no increase in money or real wages, was a tangible benefit. Most of us want that reliable, regular income, and the nearer to the end of the week or the month the more we want it. Yet non-pecuniary issues, such as status in connection with the salary, are somehow never far away from the very pecuniary issue of what we earn.

Payment of wages and salaries involves considerable organizational resources, even in small organizations. Payment on time can also require considerable effort, involving wages offices, time offices, industrial engineering departments, finance departments, computing departments and personnel departments. The co-ordination exercise can be substantial to bring these diverse elements of an organization to a regular, predictable point in time when payment is made. Many senior executives have been heard to say how they wish the effort, skill and co-ordination which result in the payment of wages and salaries could be harnessed to ensure that deliveries are made on time and output and financial targets are achieved.

How much pay and why?

Payments to employees are determined by a complex set of elements, rules, procedures, efforts and skills, to say nothing of the attributes and achievements of the individual who receives the income. Why do companies pay that person a particular income be it wage or salary and inclusive or exclusive of benefits?

Because that job or skill has historically been paid at that level?

Because that is the going rate in the area (local labour market)?

Because the rate reflects the importance of the job to the company?

Because the rate is the minimum to obtain him or her?

Because the rate is the minimum the company could get away with?

Because the level of achievement of the person justifies the rate?

Because the rate is the maximum thought to be affordable?

Because the rate seems to represent a fair level of reward?

Because the union has determined the grade or rate for the job?

Because the rate offers a certain standard of living?

Because that person at that age and with those qualifications automatically slots into such a position on a scale?

Because pay is a cost and should be minimized?

Because human beings employed in the company are assets and as such represent an important investment opportunity?

The list of possible reasons could go on and on. All the above probably operate at some time in some organizations or perhaps all organizations. The interesting point is this, surely:

THERE IS NO ONE REASON WHY EMPLOYERS PAY AN EMPLOYEE A PARTICULAR LEVEL OF EARNINGS.

On the other side of the coin, employees are receiving that level of earnings. Despite disputes, grievances, go-slows, strikes and other forms of conflict, somehow at the end of the day people accept a level of pay as their income from work. This point in the book is not the place for a complex discussion of wages theory and equilibrium in the supply and demand of manpower. But the willingness of the vast majority of employees to accept the level of payment may indicate that by whatever means of evaluation they apply they have concluded that the pay level is reasonable (whatever reasonable may mean). Why do employees accept a particular income?

Because the type of work they can do or skill they possess has always received that level of pay and no more?

Because that is the current going rate in the area?

Because they accept that the rate adequately reflects the worth of the job to the company?

Because the rate is the maximum obtainable?

Because the company/employer has the power and can get away with offering the levels of pay?

Because the employee's level of effort is being appropriately and acceptably rewarded?

Because the rate is fair?

Because that is the rate determined by the union on the employees' behalf?

Because the rate offers a certain standard of living?

Because he or she realizes that the firm is willing to invest in their talents with the prospect of improved remuneration after training?

Because that is the rate – take it or leave it?

As with the employer side of the equation the list could go on and on. But the employees' questions, which would provide for an evaluation of the rate of remuneration, somehow seem less likely than the list for the employer. Perhaps we expect the employer to provide some criteria for consideration of the labour costs they incur. Perhaps we expect much less in the way of evaluation from employees. Should we expect this situation? And is this actually the case?

A major, and admittedly contentious, assumption underlying much of the content of this book is that the overwhelming majority of employers have no clear idea of why they pay levels of remuneration to different groups of employees, and employees have no clear idea of why they settle for and accept a particular level of remuneration. In the first place there are a multiplicity of measures or evaluations which both parties can apply to income levels and other elements of remuneration.

Many will apply at one time, some will apply at different times. Usually, however, levels of remuneration which obtain in employing organizations in the United Kingdom, are parts of structures which have just grown through the influence of various pressures. Remuneration is more often than not determined by factors which are not wholly under the influence of employers and/or employees. Repeated questions from managers and employees about why they pay and accept certain levels of remuneration, usually result in replies which 'boil down' to the same answer. 'That is the pay level it has always been'; or in harsher terms, '. . . we don't really know'. There are a few organizations where the answer to the question is clear and positive.

Policy and strategy

The major reason for the uncertainty and confusion in the minds of employers on why they provide certain levels of payment is the lack of purpose for wage and salary structures. Yet these payments are important to all of us who receive them, they represent in total a considerable cost to the employing organization, and potentially represent a considerable influence on the well-being of organizations, management and employees. Given these considerations there is some substance in the argument that management need to determine much more clearly why they have a certain wage and salary structure in the interests of determining what remuneration means for the overall effectiveness of the organization. The means of developing wages and salaries structures in the interests of company effectiveness first require a policy which is linked into, and is a result of, the definition of what the company in total needs to achieve if it is to be effective. The definition of effectiveness may be taken as a variety of objectives (with accompanying controls) from profitability to quality of working life. It should be the task of the company's senior executives to determine the elements of this required effectiveness.

A policy for wages and salaries cannot be designed unless it is based on a personnel policy, and a personnel policy cannot be designed unless it is based on a company-wide or corporate policy. The word policy, as used here, means some kind of statement to provide guidance for organizational members who are in positions of responsibility and can interpret and initiate policies for the various activities of the company. With this meaning Pigors and Myers claim that a statement of policy should affirm long term aims, commit management members to take account of it, should be flexible enough to allow interpretation by managers, and be consistent with other corporate procedures.[1] The last point of consistency is perhaps the most important. Decisions in all parts of the company should be consistent with decisions made about the aims of the company, and thus consistent with one another. Personnel policy and decisions, and more particularly remuneration policy, should be consistent, for example, with production policy; a state of affairs which is achievable if both policies are aligned with one another through consistency with corporate policy. Brech described policy as some exercise in providing guidance '. . . the modes of thought and the body of principles laid down to underline and to guide the activities of the firm (or other organization) towards declared or known objectives'.[2] A policy for wages and salaries and benefits would be facilitated through such guidance in terms of the need to be supportive to the process of achieving corporate objectives. Thomason emphasizes the aspect of guidance in the following technical and moral terms:

> As such it is intended as a guide to best practice in both the technical and the moral senses. It serves to bolster the identity of the undertaking . . . by virtue of its particular modes of thought and body of principles.[3]

The technical aspect of policy introduces strategy and plan, which in turn represent a translation of a general framework of intent into operational terminology. A moral aspect refers to the behaviour of the company and its members and the level of acceptability of that behaviour to society in general, in other words a social perspective.

A strategic approach for managing remuneration

In recent years interest has increased in the use of corporate planning, operational planning and strategic planning as processes for linking managerial decision making with corporate policy. Drucker has defined corporate planning as a

> . . . process of making entrepreneurial decisions systematically . . . organizing the effort needed to carry out these decisions and measuring the results against expectations . . .[4]

This definition reveals the strategic nature of decisions within the corporate planning process. Although the strategic level may appear somewhat removed from decisions about wages and salaries, part of the effort required to carry out these decisions will involve personnel functions and therefore the management of wages and salaries. The links involved, and the implications for all aspects of the organization's work, are forged by a style of management which devotes less attention to short term issues and more attention to the longer term and more importantly the implications of current decisions. Managers should therefore think through problems, and their implications for the company, and then develop strategies to deal with those same problems.[5] It is as important for managers to adopt this approach for wages and salaries, as for the work of the company as a whole.

A strategy for wages and salaries which has a medium to long term orientation will be possible only in those organizations with a strategic perspective at the top. It is in the area of senior management that responsibility lies for an organizational climate which stimulates long term thinking, and the consideration of implications.

Finding a purpose

If strategic planning can help senior management improve the performance of the organization, and there is substantial evidence that performance is indeed improved,[6] then strategic approaches at a functional level will be determined by, and be in return supportive to, the corporate plan (*see* figure 1 below). The decisions now made about wages, salaries and benefits (along with decisions in all other areas of the company) will become strategic to the achievement of the corporate

Figure 1
Determining remuneration policy

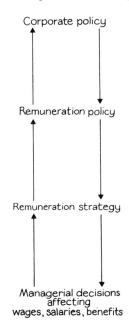

Corporate policy

Remuneration policy

Remuneration strategy

Managerial decisions
affecting
wages, salaries, benefits

plan. (Strategic decision making is taken here as the foundation of corporate planning at company level.)

To highlight the advantages of the strategic approach, we may turn to past failures and note that many wage and salary structures already contain attempts to improve employee performance in the form of incentive schemes. Many claims have been made for the effects on company performance to be derived from these schemes, but it is very difficult to find the evidence. One reason for this is that management use the scheme to determine pay only. Without a strategic approach there is no opportunity to work through an incentive scheme to the point where it demonstrably enhances company performance.[7]

Clearly there is a case for arguing that purpose can be found for the design and management of wages, salaries and benefits in the support of corporate objectives and performance. Within the strategic planning perspectives the achievement of this may be possible. But the adoption of such an approach may first require a 'sea change' in management held attitudes to the human resource.

Human asset or cost?

During the late 1960s and early 1970s some debate was attached to the subject of human resource as a cost or asset to the employer. Out of the debate came the theory of human asset accounting based on the concept of multiplying salaries and wages by factors, human asset multipliers, allocated to different job grades or groupings.[8] The end result of this process would be measures or evaluation of the human element of work comparable to the financial measures applied to physical assets. Just as the established systems of the accountant can measure changes in the value of physical assets or hardware, and indeed any return from these assets, so the systems of human asset accounting would measure changes in the human asset. Thus the underlying philosophy of this approach to the 'software' of organizations is based on a view that people are part of the organization's capital involving investment, cost and return on investment. One of the earliest, indeed originating articles on human asset accounting, by Hekiman and Jones, contained ambitious proposals involving the introduction of profit centres as the appropriate context for measuring the asset value of employees.[9] One major application of human asset accounting has been reported and involved a trial application in an American company.[10]

In recent years the impetus to develop human asset accounting appears to have weakened somewhat, probably due to the inappropriate climate of recession now prevailing in the western world. Furthermore, human asset accounting has been 'sold short'. The issue of profitability has been at odds with thinking on the system and was thus underplayed in the debate. But the major disappointment has been the priority given to the links between the technique and training and manpower planning, which has devalued the potential strength of human asset accounting to relate corporate expenditure, on a previously unmeasured element of the organization's resources, to corporate performance. Thus the relationship between remuneration and corporate performance still awaits appropriate measures.

It remains the case that human asset accounting has travelled only a short distance from the concept stage. The hope must remain that the basic assumption underlying the idea that employees are an asset to the employing organization and not merely a cost, can survive. On the basis of that hope, one can at least wish for some chance of bringing managerial attitudes round to the point where they view remuneration as an investment.

Remuneration for all reasons

With or without human asset accounting the relationship between remuneration and the organization's performance is important and worthy of attention. As in many areas of organizational life and managerial endeavour, however, it is not realistic to concentrate on one variable or one reason for decision and action. There are many forces (economic, social, technical) and a complex of theories, attitudes, beliefs and prejudices directly and indirectly capable of influencing remuneration structures and levels.

An attempt to provide a degree of administration for remuneration will be concerned with the following: government policies and actions for the economy and industry; employee demands, expectations and attitudes to work; collective bargaining and in particular the trade unions' role in the determination of remuneration levels directly and structures indirectly; the degree of rationality required by the organization's management in support of the organization task; and competitive pressures in the local labour market where manpower is recruited. Therefore, the management of remuneration becomes a process of providing direction in dealing with these influences, achieving balance between the influences and the resolution of conflict between the various interest groups which can bring pressure to bear on the organization. To shed light on the nature of this managerial process requires a consideration of the interests of those directly and indirectly involved with and affected by remuneration matters.

Government

The importance of remuneration transcends the argument that the employer should pay as little as he can get away with to maximize profits, and the employee should extract the maximum to improve and/or enhance his economic position. Remuneration is at the heart of our national economic success. Governments have a vested interest in matters of remuneration as employers of a significant part of the nation's labour force, and because pay affects the macro-economic environment. Indeed, through successive incomes policies (both official and unofficial) governments have influenced remuneration for their own employees and private sector employees. The issue of remuneration can influence the level of inflation, the incidence of disputes and strikes and the amount of money flowing around the national economy and the level of demand and consumption. Successive government policies and strategies for the economy demonstrate government concern for the impact of remuneration on the economy and have come to envelop remuneration as a tactical instrument for the achievement of government objectives. The management of remuneration requires a sensitive response to government policy and will do so for the foreseeable future.

The employee

For the employee remuneration is bound up with notions of purchasing power, standard of living, fairness or relativity and status. But the issue of what employees demand of their employers is problematical. Definitions of requirements have derived from political, economic and social perspectives which can be reduced to some idea of 'economic man' or 'behavioural man'. Another problem arises in terms of how the worker is to be perceived. Sixty years ago, Goodrich pointed to the worker in his capacity of consumer (an economic orientation) and as producer (a satisfaction orientation).[11] Work by Morse and Weiss discovered that the producer orientation predominated because it provided purpose in life.[12] Differences in orientation have been found to exist between manual and white collar employees, and Lyman concluded:

> . . . persons at the lower end of the socio-economic scale are more likely than those at the upper end to emphasise the economic aspects of work, whereas those at the upper end more typically stress the satisfaction they find in the work itself.[13]

From British research carried out during the 1960s has come evidence of

17

an instrumental orientation aligning with the view of the employee as consumer working to maximize material well-being and status rather than fulfilment at work.[14] Alongside the concern with evidence on the producer-consumer dichotomy in employee held attitudes to work the employer and remuneration, is the need to embrace the importance of the group and social considerations of work, particularly needs related to career, fulfilment and involvement.

Against this scenario of complexity in employee orientations, the management of remuneration requires a consideration of class, occupation, the nature of the basic task and technology of the enterprise and perhaps the geographical location because in the last analysis the only possible conclusion may be that work '. . . means different things to different workers'.[15] But, the money should be 'right'. This should be the first consideration from which other considerations of satisfaction, belonging and status may follow. The subject of remuneration and behavioural or social issues will be returned to in chapter 2, but for the moment we can conclude that the first facet of employee orientation, which will need a response within the remuneration offer, is the consumer or instrumental attitude.

It should not be forgotten that consumers possess indirect orientations to remuneration in their hope for increased purchasing power and their attitude to any impact of price changes on that power. The consumer may also be employee, of course, and the conflicting desires for maximum income (affecting labour costs) and competitive prices (dependent on the containment of labour costs) is an interesting one which makes the consumer-producer dichotomy an even more problematical influence on remuneration.

The employer

Remuneration represents the largest element in the value added by production. Additionally for many companies it is a significant element in the cost of production and in some cases the largest element. Therefore, the outlays on wages, salaries and benefits can be a major determinant of profitability. Much consideration has already been given to the relationship between remuneration and company performance, and it has been suggested that the managerial orientation to remuneration should be based on some desire to operationalize this relationship. Within this orientation would exist a concern with policy, strategies and tactics (or mechanisms) which result in that set of remuneration structures which can attract, retain and motivate employees in the process of pursuing corporate objectives (further attention is devoted to these issues in chapter 2). Additionally, such structures would be adaptable and equitable in the face of changing conditions, and to this end management will be concerned with dynamic economic and social factors within and without the organization.

The primacy of performance

Post-war Conservative and Labour governments have displayed a strong preference for productivity as a basis for policies influencing remuneration. This preference has risen to the surface in the clearest form within various incomes policies during the 1960s and 1970s. Government inspired statements about pay rises causing unemployment, and one man's pay rise being another man's price rise etc, have underlined government intentions (if not achievement) to influence decisions about remuneration in the interests of productivity and national economic performance.

Alongside this growing interest by government in remuneration matters, trade unions have strengthened their position in the relatively 'secure' full employment post-war years, obtaining cost of living increases and achieving, by the beginning of the 1970s, the annual bargaining round. This has been a, perhaps, ambitious pursuit of Keynes' principle of effective demand through income as the chief source of purchasing power in the economy.[16] The outcome was an inflationary spiral in the mid to late seventies resulting in managerial control of remuneration structures and their power to attract, retain and motivate employees being substantially diluted. The longer term results of this phenomenon of the 'spiral' will no doubt fill many books in the future; developments in the immediate 'post-spiral' period since 1980 indicate a return to performance as the underlying influence of remuneration policies and decisions.[17]

This performance orientation is characterized by a desire to contain unit labour costs by absorbing increases in earnings with increases in productivity and/or overall company performance. Considerations of the purchasing power of employees may now be secondary to the performance based alignment of employer, government and customer interests. To what extent this merely allows managements to develop hollow performance policies or to implement actual programmes and actions which result in tangible improvements in company performance will depend on management resolve and, more significantly (from the perspective of this book) the design and implementation of links between corporate policy, strategic thinking on remuneration, and managerial decisions about wages, salaries and benefits.

Employee orientations to remuneration may influence employer generated policies and actions only to the extent that improvements in the performance dimensions allow for sufficient flexibility to embrace employee need. Performance considerations have in the past been swept aside by the representational strength of trade unions, and the process of determining remuneration has often been a crude 'balancing act' between trade union power and employer power. Subtlety and collective bargaining have never been comfortable bedfellows. Common ground to support a performance based orientation to remuneration is still required, and there is some argument for claiming that management can and should initiate developments in this area within their approach to the 'ability to pay' dilemma.

Ability to pay

In a particular local labour market there will be a range of wage and salary levels for comparable jobs and skills. Decisions about whether to be leaders in terms of remuneration (something which most senior executives of companies wish to avoid if only because of the adverse comments from competing employers) or stay in some middle or average 'band' or maintain comparability with other companies, or pay lower than the norm, can be important determinants of remuneration policy and programmes. The financial condition, level of productivity and managerial attitudes to remuneration can be the causes of the labour market position adopted by the organization. Many shop stewards and convenors, however, consider that managerial decisions about ability to pay are unilateral and are made too often without providing the employee representatives with the facts about the financial condition of the firm.

Despite developments in some companies, 'opening the books' is not attractive to many managements, and prodding, through legislation, has generally been regarded as the means to securing change. The Employment Protection Act 1975 (s17) requires employers to respond to requests from trade unions for disclosure of company information relevant to collective bargaining. Where union requests for disclosure are not met the Advisory, Conciliation and Arbitration Service (ACAS), can become involved in a conciliation role first and an arbitration role second if conciliation fails. The course of conciliation is followed within the terms of a code of practice which covers pay and benefits, conditions of service, manpower and manning, production and sales performance, financial data and analysis. With such forms of disclosure the ability to pay may become an important determinant of the orientations to remuneration held by employers and employees. It may also provide for a movement to some agreement assuming that employee representatives accept that the financial state of the firm is an important and relevant factor. The tendency could be for unions to use financial strength, in the ability to pay consideration, to justify larger than normal increases. Just as obviously, management may rely on the ability to pay consideration in times of financial difficulty in order to press home the case for smaller than normal increases. With this in mind, we should remember that ability to pay will be dependent in the first place on managerial ability to reduce costs and enhance company performance.

It is significant that the ability to pay argument has to some extent produced a greater awareness of the need for disclosure, and the potential for a greater degree of common understanding by employers and employees on the basis of disclosure. The participative approach suggested by such a development is in turn a significant element in what should be the social context of remuneration.

Towards the acceptable remuneration

Within the discussion of influences on the structuring and the levels of remuneration, it is clear that the essential outcome is the convergence of the variety of processes and pressures to produce remunerations which are in the first instance acceptable to employers and employees and, more remotely, acceptable to customers, government and the nation as a whole. We have seen that the movement to some agreement on remuneration by employer and employee is influenced by the degree to which some compromise can be effected in the productivity and consumer orientations held by management and trade unions respectively. This move towards settlement is complicated by the presence of both productivity and consumer elements in employee orientations. Government, society and the customer will also possess orientations to remuneration which will have varying degrees of influence on outcomes. The 'stage' for settlement is the employing organization. It might be argued that the 'audience' consists of government, society and customer. But the 'play', with employer and employee representatives as the actors, must be appreciated. Such appreciation can be assured if employer and employee recognize a wider set of interests than their own. Repeated failure in this respect has resulted in increasing government intervention in the process of determining remuneration in the micro-level environment.

The process by which remuneration can be determined primarily on a performance basis is represented in outline form by figure 2 on page 22. The nucleus of this model is contained in the relationship between remuneration levels and corporate performance. Out of such a

Figure 2
Performance based remuneration

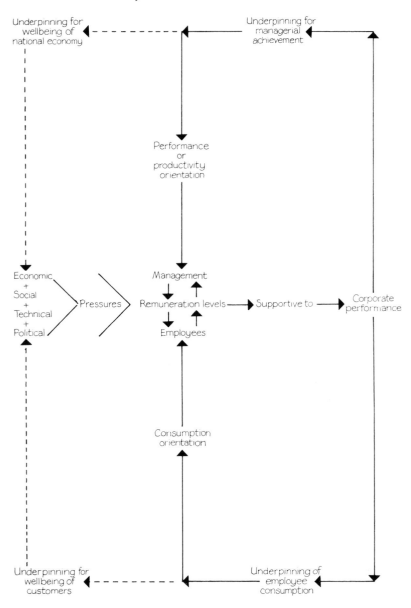

Figure 3
The dynamic model of performance based remuneration

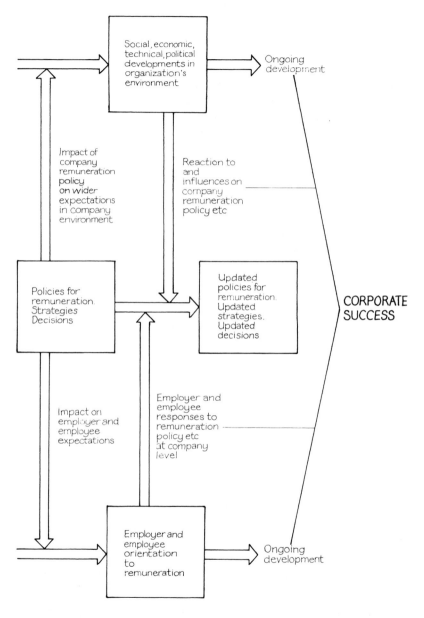

supportive relationship arise the means to underpin the consumer orientations of employees and the performance orientations of employers, and a recognition of the needs of customers (in terms of competitive prices), and the well-being of the economy. The model is presented as an ideal situation which might be strived for in the development of policy and in the management of remuneration to provide for direction, consistency and flexibility. This all takes place amidst interpretation and response to a collection of forces and philosophies which are constantly attempting to break down rationality in management and wrest control of remuneration away from managerial hands.

In figure 3 on page 23 the performance based model is developed in some detail to show how remuneration policy and management can provide this direction, consistency and flexibility.

Management and policy for remuneration

Out of the complex issues within and around the management of remuneration, it has proved possible to synthesize a primary performance based orientation in the form of links which remuneration should forge between employee performances at work and corporate performance. But achieving such links and performance objectives, represents a major task for management. It requires a management realignment with change and reality. Past technical, economic, political and social changes have outmoded traditional and respected approaches to the management of the human resource and associated matters. Changes in the technology of production and product have outpaced developments in remuneration structures so that piecework schemes, for example, have lost their effectiveness in influencing productivity. Economic forces in the form of increased price competition or increased energy costs or general inflation have found management with inflexible remuneration structures and lacking ability to contain labour costs. Political developments have seen the introduction of incomes policies, monetary policies and legislation which have created new problems for managements because remuneration structures have not coped adequately with pressures resulting in the upsetting of differentials, and restrictions on pay increases. Social changes have increased employees' desire for more information and involvement in a participative approach to the determination of remuneration. Management have responded only as a result of legislation and government generated accommodations.

These problems suggest that the management of remuneration calls for an anticipative style able to develop structures and procedures in tune with the evolving technical, economic, political and social processes which have a bearing on remuneration policy and decisions. The responses made to developments in these processes within the remuneration policy, may attempt to accommodate them in so far as such accommodations are supportive to the objectives for corporate performance.

A line management responsibility

If an anticipative style exists at the policy level, remuneration management within the organization's executive management structure should benefit. It is within that executive that line decisions about remuneration are rightly made. The specialist or staff function of personnel management will provide advice and information to and store records on behalf of the line managers. Such a situation is not always clarified in works on personnel management and in many companies there is confusion about who is and should be making decisions about human resource matters. But corporate policy and strategies rely on line effectiveness for achievement. A strategy for remuneration is no less dependent on the performance of line managers coupled with a high quality of information and advice provided to line managers by those responsible for remuneration issues in the personnel department.

Policy and implementation

A policy for remuneration should be concerned with the achievement of the following objectives:

(i) the attraction of effective employees
(ii) the retention of effective employees
(iii) the stimulation (or motivation) of these employees to work in the interests of corporate well-being.

These three objectives represent the type of contribution which remuneration should make to the operations of the organization. Their achievement requires method and effectiveness in designing remuneration structures, in determining pay levels, in providing incentives and in the provision of fringe benefits. In these ways a performance based policy has relevance to decisions which affect a crucial part of the life of organizations and their employees.

Conclusions

Remuneration plays an important role in the lives of individuals and organizations and is of importance to the well-being of the economy as a whole. It is therefore surprising to see that policies for remuneration and the managerial decisions following from that policy lack co-ordination and rationality. It is not surprising that conflict and escalating uncontrolled labour costs are often associated with such structures, particularly when managers are unable to relate elements of remuneration to the requirements for effectiveness in the total performance of the organization.

Wages, salaries and benefits can reasonably be defined as remunerations or rewards for the contributions made by employees to the performance of their employing organizations. Such a perspective may be considered conducive to a formulation of remuneration policies in the company, based on issues of performance and given direction by corporate policy. The implementation of the policy as a strategy can guide developments in remuneration and allow managerial decisions to anticipate and keep pace with changes inside and outside the firm. Around this nucleus of remuneration and performance are employer and employee orientations which need to be balanced in the pursuit of rational remuneration structures and company performance. A strategic approach can allow for this balance and the filtering through of changes in orientation by pacing and providing for managerial understanding of the economic, technical, social and political forces influencing these orientations.

The economic and social factors moulding the expectations which all of us hold about remuneration are of most immediate concern to those who would be responsible for formulating and implementing remuneration policies. Theoretical analysis and debates about these factors have been in existence for decades, indeed for centuries in the case of wage theory. Supply and demand have long been held to be at the heart of the wage determination process, at least in the opinion of economists. The supply of manpower should be equated with the organization demand if performance is to be underpinned. A discussion of theory will throw light on the contribution of remuneration to the balancing of demand and supply, and attention turns to this subject in the next chapter.

References

1 PIGORS P *and* MYERS C A, *Personnel administration: A point of view and a method*, McGraw Hill, 9th Edn. 1981. See particularly chapter 5.

2 BRECH E F, *The principles and practice of management*, Longmans Edn. 1975 p 37.

3 THOMASON G F, *A textbook of personnel management*, Institute of Personnel Management, Fourth Edn. 1981 pp 13–14.

4 DRUCKER P, *Managing for results*. Heinemann 1964.

5 TAYLOR B *and* SPARKS J R, *Corporate strategy and planning* Heineman 1977 pp 6–7.

6 TAYLOR *and* SPARKS *loc cit* p 6.

7 See SMITH I G, Why wage systems fail, in *Management Today*, July 1976, pp 44–106.

8 GILES W J *and* ROBINSON D, *Human asset accounting*, joint publication by Institute of Personnel Management and Institute of Cost and Management Accountants, 1972 p 26.

9 HEKIMAN J S *and* JONES C H, 'Put people on the balance sheet', in *Harvard Business Review*, Vol 45, No 1, January–February 1967, pp 105–13.

10 DRUMMET A L, PYLE W C *and* FLAMHOLZ E G, 'Human resource accounting in industry', in *Personnel Administration* Vol 32, No 4, 1969 pp 34–46.

11 GOODRICH C L, *The frontier of control 1920*, Penguin Books 1975.

12 MORSE N C *and* WEISS R S, 'The functioning and meaning of work and the job', in *American Sociological Review* 1955.

13 LYMAN E L, 'Occupational differences in the values attached to work', in *American Journal of Sociology* 61, 1955.

14 GOLDTHORPE J M, LOCKWOOD D, BECHHOFER F *and* PLATT J, *The affluent worker: Industrial attitudes and behaviour*, Cambridge University Press, 1968.

15 THOMASON G F *loc cit* p 158.

16 KEYNES J M *The general theory of employment, interest and money*, Macmillan 1936.

17 See particularly the publications of the Incomes Data Services Ltd, since 1979.

2
The external and internal environments

If management are willing to pay certain rates because of policy and their ability to pay, they may yet find their remuneration rates at odds with the levels obtaining in the labour market. Should managers be concerned with this problem, particularly since labour markets have been imperfectly understood for some two hundred years? The answer to this question is difficult to provide. It is true that theories of wage determination have failed to explain workings in the market but they do tell us something of the wider environment in which the management of remuneration is practised. Managers need to appreciate the characteristics of that external environment, and to this end the first half of this chapter discusses some of the major developments in wage theory and the implications for our understanding of the labour market. An appreciation of the market features does not necessarily lead to a definitive understanding. Therefore, a consideration of the features of effective remuneration within the organization may be a more fruitful basis for improving the management of remuneration. Such a consideration is contained in the second half of the chapter.

THE EXTERNAL ENVIRONMENT

The failings of classical theory

The economists' interest in wage determination has normally been concerned with the rationality and the predictability of labour supply and demand in the labour market. One such approach was the *subsistence theory of wages* which claimed that if wages rise above the subsistence level, families will increase in size, the population will increase and the supply of labour will so exceed demand that wages will be forced back down to subsistence level. The *wages fund theory* argued that wages had to be paid out of a fund from the accumulated revenues deriving from past production, and the size of fund and therefore wages were determined by the ratio of supply to amounts of revenue set aside for labour (demand). The *marginal productivity theory of wages* claimed that wages are determined on the basis of the employers' calculation of the contribution of the last worker employed, and labour is hired up to the point where there is no gain from using another unit of it. Wages therefore equal the marginal product of labour, and supply and demand will work through the labour market to ensure that equilibrium exists between wage and marginal product.

These typical classical wage theories failed to explain adequately wage determination because the reality of labour market behaviour was too unpredictable to allow for precise knowledge of how supply and demand would influence wage levels. The theories remain partial explanations at best, and underline the argument that there is no one approach but rather a multiplicity of approaches which extend beyond the traditional territory of the economist.

Thus *collective bargaining theories* have more recently been used to explain the role of trade unions in raising wage levels. These theories have relevance in the short term because they assume wage rates to be a function of the relative bargaining power of employers and trade unions at the level of the employing organization. Trade unions do influence worker decisions and therefore the supply of labour, while the employers' notions of pay are influenced by some assessment of demand. Therefore, bargaining theory tends to be like all other theories: a means of explaining how the price mechanism for labour brings supply and demand into equilibrium.

The relevance of wage theory

Despite the limitations of classical wage theory, some theories can tell us something about particular issues related to the determination of incomes. For example, marginal productivity theory tells us something about the demand for labour and the productivity issue related to wages, and bargaining theory tells us something about the interplay of employers and unions. In the last analysis, however, theories of wage determination have failed to explain how the price mechanism works in the face of a complex labour market, and have therefore not been capable of providing hard evidence to prove that the supply and demand of labour move into equilibrium.

To continue the effort to improve understanding of supply and demand within the labour market may appear, at first sight, pointless. But the need remains in the interests of improving the management of remuneration. In this way those who have a responsibility for remuneration policies, plans and programmes can acquire some appreciation of the extent to which the process influencing labour supply and demand predetermines these policies, plans and programmes. Such an appreciation requires a closer analysis of labour market behaviour.

The definition and nature of labour markets

There are two views of the labour market. It has been viewed as an abstract model in the economist's study of the supply demand and price mechanism for labour; and it has been defined by government planners as a geographical area characterized and identified by the commuting patterns of its active population. Implicit in both approaches, however, is the notion of a geographical area, and the labour market has been usefully defined by economist and planner as a 'local' labour market existing within such a definable area. (This definition does not preclude consideration of other levels, particularly the national labour market, for certain types of employee, eg professional people.) Within the market are the parties, including companies, trade unions, employees and government agencies in particular, who have major parts to play in determining market behaviour and outcomes.

The terms and conditions of recruitment and the characteristics of labour within the labour market, may divide into two distinct sectors. Dual labour market theory[1] has attempted to explain the presence of a primary and secondary labour market. In the primary sector, jobs are characterized by high wages, good working conditions, stability of employment and good career prospects. Primary sector workers are well qualified, skilled and highly productive and tend to be preferred and hired first by employers. In the secondary sector jobs have low wages, poor working conditions, high labour turnover and lack any prospects for advancement. Workers are considered to be confined to the secondary market by residence, inadequate education, training and skills, discrimination and poor work history. Jobs in hospitals, hotels and seasonal work tend to be in the secondary sector with considerable turnover, while secondary workers often include women, ethnic minorities and teenagers. The dual labour market theory has done much to throw the spotlight on the disadvantaged groups within labour markets, although the thrust of this work has been aimed at public policy rather than matters of remuneration policies in the firm.

In the last analysis, however, labour markets will be defined as follows. For employers it is that area where they recruit manpower, and for employees it is that area where they normally expect to find employment.

30

Equilibrium in the labour market

Classical wage theory assumed that the supply of labour is fixed (at least in the short term) and so is the number of employers and their 'eagerness' to employ. Thus supply and demand are assumed to converge in an equilibrium wage rate where they are equated. Given these assumptions, therefore, when wages move above the level of equilibrium, economic forces will push wages down and similarly wage levels fixed below equilibrium will be subjected to economic forces pushing them upwards. Implicit in such a view of the workings of the labour market is the notion of some kind of 'clearing' which reflects the ability of events to iron out the 'wrinkles' which are symptomatic of disequilibrium between supply and demand. Thus classical theory claims to reveal some sort of mechanism (normally a price mechanism, ie the price for labour) for directing workers from one part of the economic system to another.[2] But as Wootton pointed out, the achievement of equilibrium between the supply and demand of labour has proved difficult in practice:

> This again is a matter which can . . . become very formidable in the real world.[3]

Doubts about the notion of equilibrium, and the ability of supply and demand to clear surpluses and shortages in the labour market, were increased by the theories of Keynes who introduced the idea that wage increases could actually result in an increase rather than decrease in employment due to the stimulation of trade by wage-earners spending more. Unfortunately for Keynes, and perhaps the cause of bringing classical wage theory closer to reality, the Second World War brought about a level of employment and a reduction in unused manpower which was an unprecedented reality in line with classical theory. Thus the post-war years saw a resurgence of developed classical theories (or more appropriately neo-classical theories) for example, those of Eastham,[4] Mead[5] and Samuelson[6] among others, in which the approach to wage determination was tuned to reflect a growing concern with the consequences of monopolistic organizations for employees and employers entering the market.

As with classical theories there is a shortage of evidence to prove that neo-classical theory developments are verified in practice. It is McCormick's contention that attempts at verification have either failed because of ineffective methodology and wrong assumptions, or have resulted in a refutation of theory.[7] Even though there may be some vestigial case for allowing neo-classical theorists an opportunity for a further development of equilibrium models, there is very real doubt as to whether labour market issues can be adequately analysed by economists or at least economists alone.

The increase of intervention

The development of the labour economists' theoretical models of the labour market to embrace assumptions about institutions intervening in the market process, have introduced the administered approach to wage determination. Robinson has provided the essence of the administered model as follows:

> The actions of managements in all the companies and of the government and the trade unions together determine who gets employed where, and on what terms and conditions.[8]

Thus determination of remuneration in the firm is now seen to receive the 'artificial' influences or interventions of institutions rather than the economic theory, and has become concerned with social aspects of the intervention is deemed to take the form of such developments as improved labour market information forecasts for manpower supply and demand, and more importantly, direct intervention in the form of government policies and legislation.

The new emphasis on the possibilities of intervention to provide for the administered labour market has gone further than the boundaries of economic theory, and had become concerned with social aspects of the labour market, equity and justice. Barbara Wootton provided the following typical statement to describe the issue at the core of these developments:

> At the very least, the modern habit of assessing the value of man's work in ethical terms should carry this one corollary – that in this, as in other affairs, it matters as much that justice should be manifest as that it should be done.[9]

In the 1960s and 1970s government intervention was considered in order to achieve such justice, particularly by academics and politicians. This role for the government was operationalized in the form of the incomes policy, which represents the ultimate form of intervention to date. Rather than ensuring distributive justice, however, these 'interventions' have been basically used as regulators to stop workers by-passing the intentions of Chancellors and the Treasury. Sir Stafford Cripps, as Chancellor of the Exchequer, was to make the first peace-time attempt at a policy for incomes and prices in 1948, with decidedly mixed results.[10] A further attempt was not made until 1961 when the Conservative government decided to resort to a pay pause, and in 1962 an incomes policy statement set a norm for increases at 2.5 per cent per annum.

The Labour government came into office in 1964 on the basis of policies for growth embracing the establishment of an incomes policy. The cornerstone of Labour's policies was the intention to align incomes with productivity, and the acceptance of this performance based orientation to remuneration by government, employers and trade unions. To put those intentions into effect the February 1965 White Paper (Cmnd 2577) established the necessary machinery in the form of the National Board for Prices and Incomes (NBPI) with the power to investigate movements in prices and incomes. There were in fact no less than five incomes and prices policies from 1965 to 1970 each with a figure or norm for wage increases. The policies allowed for several exceptions to the norm, including cases where employees made contributions to increases in productivity. In fact, the productivity criterion became the primary requirement for a wage increase and the other problems were virtually ignored. This priority for productivity or performance gave rise to a wide-spread development of spurious productivity agreements as management and unions tried to find ways of circumventing the ceiling imposed by the prices and incomes policy upon pay increases.

In terms of operationalizing and achieving the desired results for a performance based incomes policy the period 1965 to 1970 must now be judged a failure. Pay increases too often outpaced the improvement of productivity, a problem by now well documented (see references 11, 12 and 13). Incomes policies and the performance or productivity criteria have remained under a cloud since 1970, and yet in one form or another they have stuck their heads above the clouds on several occasions. The Conservative government resorted to an incomes policy in 1972, although the references to performance factors were vague, and the policy was to all intents and purposes defeated by the miners' strike in 1974. A general election resulted and Labour were returned to office with a new form of incomes policy, the ill-fated Social Contract.

Since 1979 the government attempts at intervention in the labour market have employed a policy of squeeze coupled with exhortations to industry to improve performance. We may suppose that unemployment is currently assumed to be a means of controlling the collective bargaining process and the level of remuneration settlements. In the present climate, therefore, performance is likely to be associated with resource utilization. Whether this means linking remuneration to employee and corporate performance or simply reducing manpower costs by taking out large sections of the labour force is difficult to conclude.

The problems of intervention

Theories of intervention have been followed by something the early economists never enjoyed, the formulation of theory into practice with prices and incomes policies. But incomes policies have stumbled because changes in pay within the organization could not causally be related to industrial and national performance. Despite these problems an underlying desire to relate remuneration to macro- and micro-level performance remains in the debate about the national economy. To achieve such a relationship in the future may require all parties to accept that *productivity and corporate performance is the prerequisite to determining pay*, rather than assume that pay is the prerequisite to productivity and improved corporate performance.

Partial explanation and relevant issues in the economists' view of remuneration

Wage theories have been developed on the basis of assumptions which are not wholly realistic. In particular the increasing complexity and sophistication of industrial economies has shown wage theories to be simplistic and partial explanations of the workings of the labour market and the process of wage and salary determination. Nonetheless, the management of remuneration requires some reference to wage theory if only to gain an understanding of the forces in the labour market which can influence and constrain the determination of remuneration within the employing organization. To cope with these influences and constraints is an essential part of the task of managing remuneration and in turn requires attention to getting the design of remuneration right within the organization.

THE INTERNAL ENVIRONMENT

The role of remuneration inside the organization

In the last analysis the traditional forces of supply and demand, even though they are poorly understood, work imperfectly and are unpredictable, can influence what the company will pay. Demand is largely under the influence of management, supply in terms of numbers is not. Obtaining the required supply of manpower is a test for remuneration policy and decisions. Therefore, remuneration must underpin recruitment and retention. But this reflects a concern with numbers. The supply of manpower also means the contributions which employees make to their work. Therefore, the motivation of employees to work and to contribute to corporate well-being is as much a part of supply as the numbers forthcoming from the labour market, indeed it should be seen as a cornerstone of the performance orientated policy for remuneration. The objectives of such a policy may stand a greater chance of achievement if the management of remuneration concentrates on internal (organizational) elements, while attempting to understand any constraints provided by elements in the external labour market. The issues of recruitment, retention and motivation will now be studied in order to underline those areas of remuneration policy and decision where management are more likely to influence events and achieve objectives.

Recruitment

The objective for remuneration in the case of recruitment should be to attract appropriate manpower from the appropriate sector of the labour market. Gowler[14] has provided insight on the relationship between external manpower supply sources in the labour market and the internal

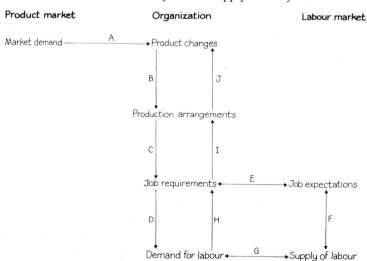

Figure 4
Determinants of labour supply to the firm

production arrangements of the firm. Figure 4 above represents the process diagrammatically. Arrow A shows how market changes can affect product changes in job requirements C and the demand for manpower D. Within these relationships remuneration should function as the 'enabler' which helps to bring forward the required manpower. In Gowler's view the process does not end here, and arrows E, F, G, H, I and J refer to the 'dynamics of the manufacturing situation'.

If the jobs (when advertised by whatever means) do not meet the expectations of the labour force in the labour market they will remain unfilled. Such expectations will include the extrinsic element of remuneration (the consumer orientation held by the worker) and the intrinsic elements of satisfaction at work (the producer orientation). Gowler argues that although the worker expectations are modified by such constraints as a scarcity of employment opportunities, it is also the case that the supply of manpower in the labour market is modified by the expectations of workers. Therefore, if the demand for manpower is not satisfied, job requirements may have to be modified (H) and in turn the production arrangements and the product programme will require modification.

A normal reaction to the above mentioned problem is to argue for the improvement of remuneration offered by the firm to overcome any resistance in the labour market. But Gowler appears to suggest that even if the firm identifies the appropriate sector of the market for recruitment purposes, behaviour in the market is not so predictable to allow any movement to supply and demand equilibrium through the mechanism of the price of labour (precisely the kind of problem discussed earlier). Thus the dynamics of the labour market (expectations, attitudes and behaviour) are social factors which defy any attempt at precision in specifying labour market outcomes in the interests of policies and decisions for remuneration. This behaviour in the market is largely beyond the influence of management. Therefore, management effort can be better used in trying to understand rather than attempting to influence market conditions.

In chapter 1 the issue of understanding the environment was discussed and presented diagrammatically in figure 3. Unfortunately this falls short of a full and co-ordinated supply of market information relevant to the management of remuneration. Only in the area of manpower planning is such material available and this is patchy.[15] Some information in the following six areas should be available however:

(i) there should be an awareness of trends in the working population
(ii) something should be known about the local recruitment situation

36

(iii)   some information should be available about industrial and employment opportunities in the area

(iv)   it should be possible to find out about rates of pay for job and skill categories by using local and national surveys

(v)   the organization should be in touch with the area's Jobcentres (local Employment Service Agency Offices) of the Department of Employment to determine numbers and skills unemployed in the local labour market

(vi)   the organization should be in touch with other employers in the area.

The information mentioned above provides only a partial understanding of the features of labour markets, and we must conclude that the management of remuneration in the firm will become all the more effective when the collection, presentation, relevance and availability of macro-level data for labour markets is improved. The reader will find a further reference to labour market information in the first part of chapter 5. More immediate improvements in the management of remuneration are available from a better understanding of, and decisions about, issues relevant to the subject of retention.

Retention

Problems in retention manifest themselves in the form of short lengths of service, particularly among young and well qualified people, high labour turnover, and a high level of absenteeism. The views taken by people towards extrinsic and intrinsic rewards, and the resultant level of retention, are impossible to accurately determine and predict. That a mix of views exists is undeniable, but their causal effect on employee behaviour is not open to conclusive analysis. Thomason has described the situation as follows:

> Some workers place prime, possibly almost exclusive weight on the monetary rewards . . . whilst others may give greater weight, by addition, to other kinds of satisfaction – security, solidarist relationships, career growth and so on. They may all 'learn' to want money as a substitute for these other kinds of satisfaction if, in accordance with learning theory, their experience persistently denies them such satisfactions. But no real situation is ever likely to present a simple black or white position on this dimension of (subjective) demand.[16]

The question of what constitutes valuable rewards in the minds of employees ought to influence management decisions about remuneration, and yet rarely does so in practice because of problems of determining what is demanded. Management are in a stronger position to determine which rewards are available, and it may be necessary to rely on a trial and error method of finding which extrinsic and intrinsic rewards, or more probably which mix of them, brings forward the desired behaviour. The 'acid test' of these experiments will be in terms of retention.

In any economic climate (and certainly in conditions of recession) people have proved to be reluctant to leave an organization if only because of a lack of knowledge of employment opportunities elsewhere in the labour market. One important piece of research carried out in Britain by Robinson, Robertson, MacKay, Gowler, Legge and Conboy and published in 1970,[17] looked into this phenomenon, and the findings are worth quoting:

> The external labour market pressures do not seem strong enough to impose a uniform wage structure in an industry . . . the firm, rather than being a helpless victim of economic forces beyond its control has a margin of opportunity within which it can adjust its internal position and take independent decisions regarding its wage structure and wage levels.
>
> Labour does not switch employment continually in order to maximize net advantages.[18]

The plain fact seems to be that employees and employers are often ignorant of the levels of remuneration paid by competing employers located in the same labour market. Retention and rates of remuneration may not, therefore, be causally related.

Despite these findings many personnel managers and line managers do attempt to base levels of remuneration on a sounding of the conditions prevailing in the external labour market. Given the problems of understanding the labour market, it is reasonable to suggest that managers might be more effective in devoting their time and efforts to determining which employee demands or needs can be met *by the firm* rather than determining extrinsic needs determined by labour market conditions, the satisfaction of which may be beyond the capacity of the firm anyway. Retention, therefore, may be more readily improved through a concern with the factors of motivation rather than the prevailing rates of remuneration in the labour market.

Motivation

When we talk of performance and contribution under the heading of supply, we are defining the kind of employee behaviour which we as managers require if corporate objectives are to have any chance of achievement. In order to bring forward this behaviour, management attempt to 'motivate' their labour force. In other words, part of the managers' task is the encouragement of employees to improve their job performance. Within policies for remuneration the word motivation is usually linked to incentives, productivity and unit costs of production. But improvements in productivity and costs are effects which are sometimes difficult to link to causes. Therefore, incentives may not always cause improved productivity.

Remuneration is not the only ingredient of motivation, and 'economic man' is not the only perspective for judging employee wants and behaviour. Yet, British managerial practice has often experienced difficulty in managing the human resource as a collection of unique individuals important in themselves rather than just as productive resources useful for achieving economic ends. Therefore, the elements of 'scientific management' dominate the management of remuneration in too many firms.

The scientific approach

Often associated with the man regarded as the founding father, F W Taylor, scientific management developed at the turn of the century as the first 'theory of management practice', and the first rationalized and organized thinking about the functions of management which had previously been at best muddled and at worst chaotic. Two points should be remembered in any debate about the worth or importance or relevance of scientific management theories:

(i) Many of our techniques and indeed much of our thinking for influencing employee work performance stems from the work of those people now collectively known as the scientific managers
(ii) British industry has seen many principles of scientific management, particularly in the areas of motivation, pay, productivity and work measurement, endure over the years, while more modern material from behavioural theory, occupational and industrial psychology hardly get a 'look in'.

Scientific management theory contained a high order of intellectual inputs and a genuine belief in industrial efficiency. But these wider qualitative dimensions have been missing from the debate and practice of management since the beginning of this century when they were developed.

Taylor believed in money or rather the bonus as a motivator, and out of his work grew the piecework bonus, an element of remuneration which has survived for decades in British industry and highlights the very limited interpretation of scientific management held by British managers. H R Pollard has summed up the issue as follows:

> It would appear that the 'body' of his ideas has grown and developed without the 'spirit'. The perfectionist attitude, the philosophy, the mental revolution died with Taylor. The techniques . . . survived and grew.[19]

This statement suggests the very fabric of remuneration management in Britain. The problems are known in every concern with outdated remuneration structures, and those concerns are many. Bonus and associated techniques represent the limit of thought and practice in too many firms, and again Taylorism in particular has so uniquely and amazingly held sway on management behaviour and practice. H R Pollard again:

> Taylor himself put the main emphasis on the bonus, the pay packet as the *motivating* factor . . . the combination of the economic theories of the nineteenth century on 'economic man' and the emphasis of scientific management on 'task and bonus' have over the past 70 years produced in most managers the firm belief that the worker is interested only in the pay packet.[20]

This seeming insensitivity to the individual's need for self-actualization, and the socio-psychological needs at the workplace, has born the brunt of criticism from behavioural scientists, who believe that such an instrumental model for management theory and practice has been at the root of industrial troubles and managerial failures. There has been some debate about Taylor's concern with socio-psychological aspects of work. He may well have been aware of their existence but offered no means of identifying and managing them. The subject was more usefully discussed by Mary Parker Follett, a much later advocate of scientific management.[21]

The behavioural approach

Remuneration is not seen as the only means to motivation in behavioural theory. Therefore, the behavioural approach considers a wide variety of influences on employee behaviour and places remuneration in context as one part of a wider strategy. The appɪ embraces many theories, among the more well known being NEɪ THEORIES, ACHIEVEMENT THEORIES, TWO FACTOR THEORY, THEORY X AND THEORY Y, SOCIAL EXCHANGE THEORY. Much of this work concentrates on issues of motivation related to job satisfaction and group structures. As with the early disciples of scientific management, there has been an over-emphasis on technique and almost a belief that the 'gates to salvation' can be unlocked if managers adopt the findings of behavioural research. It must be emphasized that the majority of original writers on the subject never envisaged such an exaggeration and abuse of their ideas.

Some examples of motivation theory

At times motivation theory in particular has been one arm of the behavioural approach which has been offered as some kind of alternative to scientific management. For example, Herzberg's motivation and hygiene theory presents such a dichotomy.[22] Motivators were defined as job factors which can increase job satisfaction and employee performance and are intrinsic to the job and the work situation. These factors include achievement, recognition, work itself, degree of responsibility and career prospects and progress. When the motivators are absent they do not depress performance, but on the other hand they are not present to stimulate a higher order of effort. Hygiene factors can prevent dissatisfaction at work but when present do nothing to improve motivation. Such factors include remuneration and working conditions. It will be clear to the reader that motivators are internal to the job and hygiene factors are external to it. Additionally, the hygiene factors could be slotted into the scientific management category. The motivation hygiene theory has been much criticized, however, particularly for failing to research thoroughly the inter-relationships between the types of motivator.

In theory X and theory Y, Douglas McGregor has provided what might be taken as an even more explicit presentation of a scientific versus a behavioural approach to motivation.[23] McGregor was convinced that by the end of the 1950s there was a body of knowledge in the social sciences which could contribute to the achievement of managerial objectives. Whatever criticisms have been levelled at McGregor's work, he made a substantial attempt to convince practising managers that social sciences had something to say of relevance to their work and objectives. Many managers have, in my experience, listened even though the practice of McGregor's ideas has been lacking. Unfortunately, discovering how to implement the recommendations of those working in the area of motivation theory appears to have been difficult to date.

McGregor's theory X is based on the 'traditional' assumptions and views of management practice, where the human resource is considered to need some degree of 'modification' to meet the organization's requirements. Thus persuasion, control, punishment and reward are used by management to overcome the resistance to and dislike of work. Such action is necessary because people are insensitive to the organization's needs, shun responsibility, strive for security and are basically self-centred. McGregor claimed that the majority of managers do in fact manage as if they believe this view of employee attitudes to be true, and because of this, employee behaviour conforms to the theory X pattern: 'Theory X explains the *consequences* of a particular managerial strategy.'[24]

The question to be asked by the reader is simple. To what extent does my organization's remuneration policy reflect the elements of theory X? To what extent does the wage and salary structure of my organization persuade, control, punish and reward employee behaviour?

If theory X can be claimed to have its roots in the motivation theory deriving from scientific management, theory Y can be seen to have roots in the motivation theory arm of behavioural theory. The assumptions of theory Y revolve around the workers' untapped willingness to accept change and his need to work for organizational objectives. Thus managers do not have to intervene through persuasion and the like because the motivation to succeed already exists within people, and will be realized if management provide objectives to which people can feel committed and in the achievement of which employees can recognize and develop their potential.

Perhaps the main conclusion to be derived from McGregor's theory Y is the requirement for management to develop new conditions, structures and processes in which employees can find the opportunity to tap their potential abilities and contribute to the organization's performance. If such conditions exist as a context for remuneration policy, perhaps we may assume that the contributions of remuneration to employee motivation can be maximized.

Although his work has been heavily criticized, we should remember that McGregor is suggesting a *direction* for thought and action. That is the most important platform of all motivation theory: to suggest, indeed provide some general direction and a basis for further analysis and discussion. If behavioural theories could be accepted in this light, particularly by managers, rather than be ignored as untenable and exaggerated claims, then the long overdue renaissance in the practice of managing the conditions of motivation in British industry might be realized.

Significance for management

Goldthorpe, Lockwood, Bechhofer and Platt examined the expectations of workers in three factories in the Luton area, arguing on the basis of their research findings that work '. . . is a means (instrument) to some other end – like living – and can have chiefly expressive functions only exceptionally'.[25] This conclusion contrasts starkly with the work of behavioural theorists. The alignment of the instrumental perspective with some of McGregor's theory X assumptions, particularly reward, which becomes the major or sole influence of worker involvement, commitment and motivation to the job is notable. Within the capitalist society the working man's alienation from the non-instrumental elements at work has been emphasized and in the words of Goldthorpe *et al*: '. . . all work activity in industrial society at least, tends to have a basically instrumental component'.[26] But is this component sufficiently large or dominant to oust social considerations in the workplace? People do work for reasons additional to remuneration; they need to belong to groups, have needs for security and need a permanent and structured way of daily life. The needs of the ego should also be remembered. Such needs exist to varying degrees within most people, but they do not depress the individual's need for remuneration.

Financial *and* behavioural elements have a bearing on motivation at work. In the management of remuneration it is essential to get the right balance between the two.

That pay has dominated the issue of motivation in industry is one half of the main thesis of this discussion of motivation. That this dominance has resulted in an over-reliance on techniques at the expense of professionalism, justice, managerial competence and respect by workers for managers must be the other half. This is not to say that pay as such is over-emphasized, but that other non-pecuniary issues are too often neglected. If they are attended to and 'mobilized' along with the pecuniary issues then the result could be a synergistic effect where employee and company performance benefit.

A spectrum of needs

It may be necessary to get the remuneration right first, but remuneration meets only part of a spectrum of worker needs, and when it is judged to be right by the worker, may give rise to other needs becoming the dominant influence of worker behaviour. If not met, then

43

frustration of these other needs will depress worker behaviour. The clearest presentation of this phenomenon was provided by Maslow, who postulated that once the 'lower order' physiological needs of the individual are satisfied, the 'higher needs' such as esteem and belongingness emerge with greater predominance in the process of influencing behaviour.[27]

In testing Maslow's thesis Alderfer claimed to have found three basic needs (the ERG Theory):[28]

EXISTENCE which includes physiological security and material desires.

RELATEDNESS which involves belonging to groups such as the work group and provides for interaction.

GROWTH which includes those needs concerned with creativity and contribution which stretch the individual and require him to extend his capacity for work.

To some extent these needs parallel Maslow's hierarchy model, and it is interesting to note that the satisfaction of the instrumental need EXISTENCE comes first and increases the potency of the other needs. Additionally, failure to satisfy high order needs may cause regression to the lower order needs. If GROWTH needs are not met concern about remuneration may increase.

We may conclude that there is a requirement to *balance* elements of remuneration with the social elements of working life if remuneration is to motivate a workforce successfully. But this balance must provide for equity within the remuneration system, for equity is an inevitable part of the employee's motivating environment.

Equity

It is not total pay which excites people but pay comparisons. Comparability is at the heart of the equity issue, and relative pay can be a frequent cause of industrial relation disputes. Weaving through the discussion of the subject are notions of what constitutes fair pay, although such discussions would comfortably fill a book on their own.

Perceived equity

A discussion of equity in remuneration brings in the three issues of recruitment, retention and motivation. An over concern with recruitment can create problems in terms of equity in remuneration structures. The need to attract and recruit manpower should be balanced with the need to avoid causing problems in the areas of motivation and retention through the maintenance of 'distributive justice' among the existing workforce. The willingness of people to stay in the organization and, more importantly perhaps, their level of contribution to company performance, are more dependent on 'relative' levels of remuneration than absolute levels. Indeed the motivational and equity factors are inextricably intertwined as influences on worker behaviour and performance. Lawler and Porter have discussed the notion of 'perceived equity' as a factor which is a significant influence on job satisfaction. The diagram below presents this role for 'perceived equity'.

Figure 5
Based on a theoretical model for the relationship between job satisfaction and performance

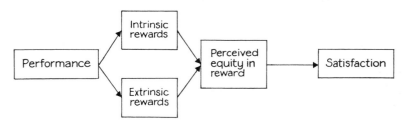

Source: Lawler and Porter, *Industrial Relations*, Vol 7, No 1, 1967

In Lawler and Porter's model, 'perceived equity' in the financial reward is both consequence of performance and cause of satisfaction. Satisfaction at work is therefore dependent on the degree of equity perceived in the reward by the employee. Homans highlighted the serious consequences of a failure to provide for 'perceived equity' or 'distributive justice':

> The more to a man's disadvantage the role of distributive justice fails to realization, the more likely he is to display the emotional behaviour we call anger and . . . they also learn to do something about it.[29]

That 'something' in Homans' words probably exists at the least in the form of comparability disputes and days lost and production lost through strikes and other less newsworthy sanctions.

Timm[30] has suggested that reactions to perceived inequity include toleration of any distress caused; the demand for compensation as restitution; retaliation against causes of inequity; rationalizing the inequity; withdrawal from the situation where inequity is perceived. The supporting evidence for these reactions may be somewhat thin but tends to suggest that motivation and retention in particular suffer heavily from perceptions of inequity with absenteeism, increased turnover, expressed dissatisfaction with the job and reduced effort and performance being the main indicators of the presence of perceived inequity.[31]

Equity, management and comparability

Unfortunately justice, fairness and equity are variables which are immensely difficult to measure. Additionally, people's perceptions differ, for example, one man's perception of justice may be another man's perceived injustice. Mankind does not come up to British Standard Specification and notions of fair reward differ from person to person. Thus, the distribution of remuneration is a difficult exercise and is unlikely to avoid problems of controversy and dispute completely. The evidence presented above argues that equity deserves serious consideration by management to minimize problems which depress employee performance. In the main, such problems will arise through the comparability 'test'.

An employee judges the degree of equity in his or her remuneration by comparing it with that of other employees in the company and with employees doing similar work in the industry or labour market (if he or she possesses the information). Additionally, when the employee compares his remuneration with that of other skills or grades within the company he may perceive the degree of equity in terms of ranking within the various levels, and perhaps, the differences in amount between the rankings (see section Two). Comparability of effort will also be tested by the employee if he is involved in a productivity based incentive scheme. His level of effort should bring forward a clearly related and defined level of bonus determined by work measurement (see section Three). The employee's perceived equity here will be determined by comparisons of his own level of bonus and level of effort with those of others within the incentive scheme. Therefore, equity is bound up with notions of the worth of a job and the worth of effort in the minds of employees.

The multiplicity of issues for remuneration

The role of remuneration in the attraction, retention, motivation and provision of perceived equity to employees is both important in itself, and in the way it is linked to non-pecuniary factors which have an equally important role to play. In the early days of management theory, the work of those collectively known as the scientific managers

emphasized the isolation of the monetary element in attracting, retaining and motivating a labour force. Unfortunately, this perspective has tended to hold sway in the practice of managing remuneration systems. The result has been remuneration systems which have become outmoded, particularly by social developments outside and inside the firm.

Remuneration is a reward which needs to be accompanied by other types of reward, particularly if remuneration is to be effectively deployed as a means of retaining and motivating people and minimizing their perceived inequity. Wages, salaries, company cars, pensions and the like should be 'mixed in' with status, job satisfaction and other behavioural elements in a synergystic effect which brings forward the required levels of effort and/or contributions from employees.

Conclusions

In this chapter we have seen that the organization's performance orientated remuneration policy operates within the constraints of poorly understood forces working in the external environment of the labour market. These forces include supply and demand for manpower, the processes of collective bargaining and government policies. In the main they are outside the influence of the managers within the organizations. Nonetheless, management should appreciate the existence of the forces, should remember that responses will be necessary at times (for example to the introduction of incomes policy) and most important should design remuneration structures within the organization which can adequately cope with and survive the impact of unpredictable labour market forces.

To ensure survival in the face of uncertainty requires the forging of links between corporate and employee behaviour. This link can be considered as a contract (material and psychological). In operating the contract policy, programmes of action and decisions for remuneration seek to attract, retain and motivate employees. These are three building blocks for the policy and management of remuneration in the organization. Equity is the cement which holds these blocks together as a viable integrated remuneration system. In the practice of the management of remuneration, attention to the structure of remuneration, the provision of incentives and of fringe benefits will be the means to minimizing problems in the areas of attraction, retention, motivation and equity. The reader will find these matters discussed in depth in the remainder of this book.

References

1 See DOERINGER P B and PIORE M J, *Internal labour markets and manpower analysis*, Heath Lexington Books 1971. Also CRAIG C, RUBERY J, TARLING R, and WILKINSON F, *Labour market structure, industrial organization and low pay*, Cambridge University Press, 1982, particularly chapters 5 and 6.

2 WOOTTON B, *The social foundations of wage policy*, Unwin Books, 2nd Edn., 1962, p 15.

3 *Ibid.*

4 EASTHAM J K, *An introduction to economic analysis*, English Universities Press, 1950, p 207.

5 MEADE J E, *Economic analysis and policy*, Oxford University Press, 1937, 2nd Edn.

6 SAMUELSON P A, *Economics*, McGraw Hill, 1948.

7 McCORMICK B J, *Wages*, Penguin 1969, chapter 2.

8 ROBERTSON E J, Local labour markets and plant wage structures: an introduction, in *Local labour markets and wage structures*, D Robinson ed, Gower Press, 1970, p 17.

9 WOOTTON B, *loc cit*, p 190.

10 LYDALL H F, 'Inflation and the earnings gap', in *The labour market*, D J McCormick and E O Smith eds, Penguin, 1969, pp 336–43.

11 TURNER H A, 'Collective bargaining and the eclipse of incomes policy: Retrospect prospect and possibilities', in *British journal of industrial relations*, July 1970, pp 197–212.

12 McKERSIE R B, and HUNTER L C *Pay, productivity and collective bargaining*, Macmillan 1972, chapter 4.

13 BALFOUR W Campbell, *Incomes policy and the public sector*, Routledge and Kegan Paul, 1972, p 225.

14 GOWLER D, Determinants of the supply of labour to the firm, *Journal of Management Studies*, Vol 6, No 1, 1969, pp 73–95.

15 SMITH I G, *Personnel Review*, Vol 11, No 3, 1982, pp 3–10.

16 THOMASON G F, *A textbook of personnel management*, Institute of Personnel Management, Fourth Edn, 1981, p 154.

17 ROBINSON D ed '*Local labour markets and wage structures*', Gower Press 1970.

18 *Ibid* p 268.

19 POLLARD H R, *Developments in management thought*, Heinemann, 1974 p 14.

20 *Ibid* p 15.

21 METCALF H C *and* URWICK L *eds The collected papers of Mary Parker Follett*, Management Publications Trust, Pitman 1957.

22 HERZBERG F, *Work and the nature of man*, World Publishing 1966. Also 'One more time: how do you motivate employees?' *Harvard Business Review on Management*, Heinemann, 1976.

23 MCGREGOR D *The human side of enterprise*, McGraw Hill 1960.

24 *Ibid* p 42.

25 GOLDTHORPE J H, LOCKWOOD D, BECHHOFER F *and* Platt J, *The affluent worker: Industrial attitudes and behaviour*, Cambridge University Press 1968, p 38.

26 *Ibid* p 41.

27 MASLOW A H, *Motivation and personality*, Harper Bros, 2nd Edn, p 38.

28 ALDERFER C P, *Existence, relatedness and growth: Human needs in organizational settings*, Free Press, New York, 1972.

29 HOMANS G C, *Social behaviour: Its elementary forms*, Harcourt, Brace and World, 1961, pp 232–233.

30 TIMM P R, Worker responses to supervisory communication inequity: An exploratory study, *The Journal of Business Communication*, 16, 1978, pp 11–24.

31 See particularly POTCHEN M, 'Absence and employee feelings about fair treatment', *Personnel Psychology*, 13, 1960, pp. 349–360. DITTRICH J *and* CARRELL M R, 'Dimensions of organizational fairness as predictors of job satisfaction, absence and turnover', *Academy of Management Proceedings*, 1976, pp 79–83. Also TIMM *loc cit*.

Part II

STRUCTURE AND DESIGN

3
The issue of structure

Remuneration structures are made up of many components which exist because of the lack of strategy and which have grown in importance because of management's concern with short term problems. Without purpose and strategy, rationality and principles give way to *ad hoc* adjustments to pay in response to immediate pressures. These adjustments take place in many forms and for many reasons; but the result has been complex structures that have moved outside the influence of management and have become a threat to managerial control of labour costs. Only through some understanding of the problems, issues and pressures involved will management begin to effect improvement. The acquisition of such an understanding has often been secondary to an acquisition of techniques to deal with the situation. Thus many employing organizations have turned their attention to job evaluation in particular, to 'turn round' the process of decay in pay structures. Below is a discussion of the characteristics of current remuneration structures and the reasons why they have become difficult to manage. It examines the extent of the problem and the nature of the task facing the design of techniques which may help to effect some improvement. Following this is a discussion of the role of job evaluation in the design of pay structures.

Complexity in pay structures

There are too many elements which make up the wages and salaries paid in the majority of British employing organizations. The problem is particularly acute with blue-collar groups, because their pay reflects more aspects of working conditions than is the case with white-collar groups. At the very least, a shop floor operative's pay may consist of the following:

(i) the nationally agreed time rate or basic rate for the industry
(ii) overtime payments

(iii) bonus payment paid within the terms and conditions of a payment by results scheme

Additionally the follow payments may be included:

(iv) shift-working premiums

(v) allowances for tools, specialist operations, being on standby, abnormal working conditions, clothing and footwear, first aid duties, firefighting duties, providing instruction, travel mileage and transport, meals subsistence and lodging when working away from the normal place of work, a telephone allowance and luncheon vouchers

It is not uncommon in the engineering and associated industries for national time rates to be accompanied by the following:

(vi) local area negotiated addition to basic pay

(vii) Factory/plant level negotiated addition to basic pay, such as payments for attendance or straight time rate supplements.

It is possible, therefore, to identify at least seven components in the blue-collar worker's pay packet. Much of this has been the result of the fragmented and uncoordinated nature of collective bargaining in the United Kingdom. The industry-wide or national agreement is not the only determinant of wage packet contents and companies often choose to bolster or supplement national agreements with local area bargains and factory bargains struck with union district officials.

The high incidence of premium payments, such as overtime and bonus, is also particularly British, and again stems from the archaic nature of our industrial relations systems. They make up for nationally determined pay levels which have come to be regarded as providing an unacceptably low standard of living.

With so many tiers of payments the result is a complex and confusing wage and salary structure which is difficult to administer, and which contributes to poor industrial relations and low levels of employee motivation because every element of pay can and does become an opportunity for dispute. Nationally determined basic pay provides enough distraction from the management of remuneration. The addition of local disputes, shop floor battles with the rate-fixer about bonus and battles with the foreman about the allocation and rates for overtime only complicates the process further. Nor are such industrial relations problems limited to the elements of shop floor pay. Overtime and merit payments readily give rise to disputes between management and white-collar employee representatives.

Within each tier of payment a considerable variety of provision can exist. Overtime payments can be paid at time and a quarter (basic or national rate plus 25 per cent); or time and one third (basic + $33\frac{1}{3}$ per cent); time and one half (basic plus 50 per cent); or double time, depending on the day the overtime is worked or depending on the company, the department or the section involved! Normal practice provides basic plus 25 or $33\frac{1}{3}$ per cent for weekday evenings, basic plus 50 per cent for Saturday and double time for Sunday and national holidays.

Bonus payments and merit payments (or incentive payments) are paid for a predetermined level of employee performance. It is impossible to define any standard size of bonus, although the majority seem to lie in the range five to 40 per cent of basic pay. The smaller bonuses are usually paid to white-collar groups, with the largest going to direct production workers. With piecework schemes, bonuses can differ from individual to individual, and it is quite common to find a variety of bonuses in companies operating incentive schemes.

Rather more standardization characterizes the element of shift payments within firms, although amounts vary from firm to firm depending on the shift pattern. Night work may be paid at a higher rate than an evening shift. A scale of shift payments may be used to reflect the number of shifts per week, and the differences in the amount of unsocial hours. An example is the paper and board industry which currently pays at the following five levels (Incomes Data Services Report 372, 1982):

Daywork
Doubledays
Staggered days
3 shift
4 shift

Alternatively a scale of payments may be used for different skill levels or levels or responsibility. The payments for shift working are usually less prone to dispute than overtime and bonus payments.

Allowances normally account for a small proportion of pay but somehow seem to cause friction between management and employees out of all proportion to their financial value. This may be due to the employees attitude that allowances are their's by right, and care is needed in their allocation. To give some idea of the size of payments, the following are typical figures taken from some 1982 manual pay settlements:

Board and lodging—£9.50 per night

55

Responsibility—12p to 20p per hour

Possession of Certificates for specialist work (eg welding)—13p to 28p per hour

Daily travel allowance—60p to £6.50 depending on distance

Abnormal conditions—15p to £2.50 per day

Standby allowances—£2.50 to £7.00 per day depending on day of week and whether a holiday

Beer allowance—2 pints per day!

These examples are offered as some illumination on the subject rather than as a guide.

The provision of local and factory supplements to the basic or time rate has declined in recent years, but the trend is now being reversed by the introduction (through negotiation) of attendance allowances. Two examples of these payments in 1982 agreements are:

Chemicals firm West Yorkshire—£15.90 per month

Photographic materials Home Counties—£5.43 to £8.90 per week according to grade.

The current growth in popularity of these allowances prompts the view that the fragmentation of pay structures is likely to remain a permanent characteristic of the remuneration exercise, despite temporary attempts to consolidate them and premium payments. (Should the reader dispute that such complexity and confusion exists, the yellow pages of the Incomes Data Services monthly reports will quickly dispell any doubts.) The problems and the issue of structure deserve careful consideration. Managerial weakness is a prime reason for remuneration structures which are confusing and unmanageable.

Failing remuneration structures

It is not uncommon to discover line managers who should be aware and yet are unaware of the remuneration levels and differentials within their companies (a dismaying state of affairs which often leads to management weakness and disadvantage in the collective bargaining process). Furthermore the influences on remuneration can be outside managerial control. Management may have been unable to resist the pressures in the labour market, and the bargaining power of key groups of employees. Or they have been unable to control bonus and overtime earnings, or unable to initiate change and obtain employee agreement on new remuneration structures to replace those which are outmoded and ineffective. Thus pressures of the moment influence pay, rather than managerial purpose related to some long term strategy.

The realization that remuneration structures are no longer appropriate and effective usually stems from grievances based on comparability of job rates by the workforce. In other words, not only are remuneration structures irrelevant to corporate need; they are irrelevant to the needs and expectations of employees. Indeed, job evaluation can be requested by shop floor representatives before management have considered the basic problem to be solved. Problematic pay structures impact upon the workforce as much, if not more than they impact on management. But usually, the problems stem from managerial decisions relevant to the short term without regard to the long term implications.

Managerial decisions on recruitment may emphasize high and attractive remuneration levels now (to remain competitive in the labour market) at the expense of upsetting pay relativities within the organization in the longer term. Peoples' preferences (or prejudices) may influence the particular worth placed on a job by the company, and such worth will reflect subjective views rather than any recognition of the requirements for effective structure. Feelings, beliefs and attitudes have proved to be means of determining pay and those soon lead to conflict on the subject of what is an equitable remuneration for the job. In conditions of inflation, cash flow problems, changing technology, reorganization, more competitive markets and demanning, it becomes difficult for management to appreciate where remuneration issues are leading. Thus pay determination can become a 'free for all' resulting in totally inappropriate priorities for remuneration, which in time lead to grievance and dispute. In difficult and unpredictable environments subjective opinions can reign supreme, resulting in wage and salary structures which to all intents and purposes appear irrational and irrelevant to the objectives and conditions facing the company.

Overtime

In recent years some industries have seen very real attempts to reduce the amounts of overtime working.[1] This reverses the trend of the post-war years which resulted in British industry working more overtime than any other industrial nation. Much of this overtime has been un-necessary and systematic, worked as a regular arrangement to provide an acceptably sized pay packet, rather than to meet the requirements of the job.[2] There is an amazing pattern to overtime working and high levels can often be traced to the same industries, firms, departments and even individuals. This is because a high incidence of overtime is

57

associated with low basic wage rates. People who work overtime rely on its availability for a large proportion of their pay packet and the weekly budget is based on its availability. Thus the expectation and working of a particular amount of overtime becomes a convention which is difficult to change, a phenomenon which has been termed 'policy overtime'.

During the 1960s and early 1970s, much research was carried out on overtime working, particularly as a result of the work of the National Board for Prices and Incomes and the Royal Commission on Trade Unions and Employers' Associations. Many interesting practices were revealed by the research, for example 'Welting' in the Liverpool docks and 'Spelling' at Glasgow docks, where only half the 'gang' would work on the vessel at any one time, each half working one hour on and one hour off. In the shipbuilding industry, weekend overtime could be worked by all the men working on the ship on Friday regardless of the number of men actually required for the weekend work. A strict imposition of rules for overtime was discovered in the building industry with people paid the overtime premiums regardless of whether or not they had work to do in the overtime hours. In these ways, the working of unnecessary overtime has become a permanent part of the pay structure. It represents a form of normatively-controlled behaviour sanctioned by a management willing to allow it to happen for the immediate objectives of peace on the shop floor, attractive rates for recruitment and the retention of certain employee groups.

A phenomenon often connected with overtime working is the opportunity for the foreman to dictate the company's pay policy at shop floor level because he determines who will work overtime. Thus a significant element of an employee's pay packet is not determined by a centrally co-ordinated company policy based on the real requirements of work, but on the whims, preferences and weaknesses of the shop-floor supervisor.

Some overtime working may be inevitable, for example maintenance staff staying beyond shift to complete essential repairs to machinery or a production department coping with a rush order. The question to be asked, therefore, is not 'should overtime be worked at all?', but rather, 'can overtime working be reduced to the absolute minimum necessary for the company's operations and do we need to pay for it?'. To remove overtime payments is to remove a major cause of distortions in payment rates and, therefore, a cause of comparability disputes and grievances about the fairness of overtime distribution. Attempts to consolidate overtime payments in an overall rate became popular in the 1960s with the advent of productivity agreements.[3] During the 1970s, overtime working became a ploy to overcome the limitations on pay set by incomes policies, but recent evidence suggests a trend to reduce the amount of overtime pay, particularly in the engineering and chemicals industries. Interestingly, in the summer of 1981 the TUC published guidelines on shorter working hours including the following statement:

> ... eliminating overtime over a period of years by progressively tightening these limits (on overtime) or phasing in overtime reductions with annually negotiated increases in basic pay.[4]

Such a move would not only increase managerial control of pay structures, but tidy up such structures in the interests of greater rationality. However a cautionary note needs to be added here. Many exercises in reducing overtime have been part of a harmonization process designed to bring pay methods into some kind of harmony between white collar and manual staffs. This has usually involved an increase in basic pay with an appropriate reduction in overtime rates. Although a reduction in overtime working has sometimes been achieved, the elimination of a variety of rates has not, and overtime payments continue as fragmented parts of the remuneration package.

A new complication

The discussion of overtime assumes more significance when developments in job sharing, part-time and temporary work arrangements are considered. Overtime working could disappear as it is absorbed into job sharing, with one man's overtime payments becoming another man's basic earnings.

In the wider context of remuneration structures any increase in job sharing and part-time working may well increase the number of pay components. If we assume that the level of overheads are to be maintained (if not decreased) in the current climate of recession there will be no more money in the system with the result that current remunerations will be split across the job sharing employees. Thus the opportunities for creating anomalies and perceived inequity are likely to increase with such developments. Whatever the practical arguments may be for and against job sharing and the like, there can be little doubt that the implementation of such methods will increase rather than reduce the complexity of remuneration and its management. The redistribution of pay-roll elements, the determination of new wage and salary structures, the re-jigging of benefits and premium payments are a few of the problems which may face management who choose to adopt job sharing. Solutions to the problems are of course possible, but arriving at them will be an agonizing task, which many executives would prefer to avoid. For them government legislation may be the only means

59

to introducing job sharing, and that in turn may depend on attitudes to unemployment. Obviously this is an indeterminate issue, but one which will greatly affect the management of remuneration should it gain in significance.[5]

Wage drift

An all too familiar distortion in remuneration structures is wage drift: the tendency for wages actually paid at the work place to rise at a rate which is faster than that arranged by agreement between management and union representatives. Overtime and payment by results are the main causes of wages drifting away from levels determined within a structure, although opinion has generally held payment by results (PBR) to be the most significant cause. In 1968 the National Board for Prices and Incomes concluded:

> ... the most important element in wage drift is represented by increases in piecework or incentive earnings which are not necessarily connected with greater effort.[6]

In these terms wage drift can be considered to be some kind of breakdown in the supposed causal relationship between earnings and effort. The level of pay actually received by the operative drifts upwards and away from the level of pay agreed within the structure of bonus earnings and based on pre-determined levels of effort. This sort of drift is a serious problem, not just for remuneration structures, but in terms of the inflationary consequences. Actual earnings which bear no relationship to earnings levels within jointly agreed remuneration structures are outside managerial control. They are unpredictable, difficult to calculate quickly, and represent costs which are not offset by productivity. There are five main ways in which PBR contributes directly to wage drift.

Change and incentives—Because incentive schemes attempt to link earnings and output they are vulnerable to the effects of increasing automation in operations and tasks. These push up output and therefore earnings without any contribution from the employee. Needless to say, those involved in work not affected by technological change will soon feel aggrieved. Such problems can be difficult to solve because management cannot adjust incentive payment levels for every change affecting every individual task and operative. This is particularly the case in firms with complex production systems where changes in methods, equipment and materials are continuous.

The learning curve phenomenon is a further feature of PBR which describes the way in which output in a particular task rises steadily over time without any change in the task itself and without any increase in worker contribution to output. Sometimes this happens because workers increase their skill and learn short cuts in the task method in order to increase earnings. Sometimes the cause is an accumulation of individually undetectable improvements in the task itself.

Pieceworkers' 'creep' occurs when piece rates are repeatedly and frequently changed through the process of negotiation. This quite often occurs with employee groups who are in a position to pressure management. Shop floor representatives will press for increases in the incentive payments regardless of the levels of worker effort on the grounds that total output has increased. Management face some difficulty in coping with these pressures and arresting or reversing the process of 'creep', because of strong union organization on the shop floor and their inability to analyse events within the production process which will allow for a precise measure of labour's contribution to output. Such a measure has been needed for a few decades as a means for providing management with a convincing counter argument to shop floor claims on pay and performance.

The 'ratchet phenomenon' describes the negotiation of specific agreements for payment by results schemes for limited periods with a tendency for each new agreement to contain higher incentive payment levels than those applying in the previous period. Such increases may bear no relation to effort and productivity, and thus collective bargaining pressures and strong unionized representation culminate in the upward 'ratchet' effect movement of earnings.

An indirect contribution to drift is provided by PBR because earnings are unevenly distributed among groups of workers causing pressure for increases from those groups who have not fared too well. Employee groups such as white collar and supervisory staffs will readily seize upon these inequities to substantiate their claim for a pay increase which will bring them back into line with trends set by employees on PBR. The main causes of this type of leap-frogging include differences in working conditions, differences in work load, differences in the length of production runs, differences in the frequency of changes in method and task and differences in the type and size of incentive payments. These situations can cause 'felt inequities' and 'actual inequities' between groups covered and groups not covered by PBR, and between groups of employees covered by the same or different PBR schemes.

The drift associated with incentive schemes stems from circumstances on the shop floor, at the point of application of the measurement exercise and the bonus payments. The relationship between earnings, effort and output somehow seems to break down in the conditions of the work place. The technical niceties which form the work measurement based levels of effort, the assumed link between effort and pay and the assumed relationship between effort and productivity (or company performance) are made ineffectual by what are mainly social pressures from the shop floor. These social pressures have found expression in the shop floor bargaining exercises which characterize too many incentive schemes and normally involve shop steward, foreman and work study people in small 'battles' which push earnings ever upwards regardless of any measure of effort and output. Thus actual labour costs come to bear no relationship to the expected costs based on the formal and negotiated remuneration structures. The difference between expected labour costs and actual labour costs is the amount of wage drift in the organization. Even in companies with achieved and consistent high levels of increase in productivity, the growth has often been insufficient to contain rising labour costs with wage drift continuing to push up production costs.

In terms of remuneration, wage drift is a breakdown of structure resulting in perceived inequity, depressed motivation and uncontrolled labour costs. For the moment, it is necessary to emphasize that earnings should be under some form of managerial control (the form of that control may be unitary or participative, a subject worthy of considerable attention in isolation) if structures are to work and thus avoid problems of comparability, leapfrogging and drift. As far as PBR is concerned this control should be based on corporate requirements for total productivity, rather than the rate-fixers' subjective measurement of effort expended in an individual's task. The history of remuneration in British industry points to the need for direction derived from corporate policy and a strategic approach to the management of remuneration.

Labour costs and drift in much of British industry continue to be serious problems, lacking effective solutions. Such solutions cannot be found in the techniques of job evaluation and payment by results in isolation from management objectives. Techniques can work if they are related to corporate requirements through line management decisions about performance and the consequent implications for remuneration structures. Failure to do this in the past has left many companies in worse rather than better situations after introducing job evaluation and PBR schemes, and there are too many line managers disillusioned with these techniques.

Merit bonuses

Incentive payments and overtime payments are premiums which represent an addition to basic pay. Although white-collar incentive schemes and overtime in the office are frequently found, a popular premium payment for white-collar staffs has been the merit bonus. Unlike the shop floor PBR scheme which attempts some measure of worker effort and/or productivity, the merit scheme is based on the supervisor's opinions of an employee's personal qualities in such areas as timekeeping, dilligence, responsibility, co-operativeness and adaptability. As with PBR, relating merit to pay can be notoriously difficult given the subjectivity of the assessment. Those not on a merit scheme may feel disadvantaged, and there may be serious differences in the levels of payment arising from nothing more substantial than supervisor preferences and prejudices. Merit schemes are often used for the best of reasons, but like the other initiatives discussed in this chapter, represent an opportunity for management to introduce differences in payment levels which can ultimately lead to distortion and failure in remuneration structures.

Comparisons between organizations

It is frequently possible to find a wage and salary structure which the organization has copied from some other enterprise. This may result from management's eagerness to remain competitive in the labour market, alternatively, management may wish to maintain some form of comparability with other firms in the industry, or to 'toe the line' with other employers in a local and well organized employment area. Invariably such structures become unsuitable for the organization's internal circumstances and objectives with the passage of time, and conflict occurs unless management adjust rates to reflect new circumstances. These adjustments usually introduce unnecessary complexity and inequity to what may already be inappropriate and unmanageable structures.

The question of comparability of remuneration between companies is often in the forefront of management thinking, and job evaluation exercises across firms, usually within a particular industry, have not been unknown. Lupton and Bowey have presented an interesting approach to interfirm evaluation for use in the collective bargaining process.[7] In the main, however, companies attempt comparisons through national salary surveys, management consultant surveys and surveys prepared by groups of employers on behalf of member organizations. The major uses of this information are to keep management informed of rates offered by employers competing in the same labour market, and to provide information for the collective bargaining exercise.

Strength and weakness in bargaining

A pressure which tends to 'bend' remuneration structures is the relative bargaining strength of some groups of employees and the relative weakness of management to resist the pressure, particularly where they feel vulnerable to strike action, because sales and receipts and therefore cash flow will be adversely affected. In a large organization with multiple divisions and tasks, management acceptance of one group's demands can quickly lead to other groups demanding comparability or indeed leapfrogging over one another in an upwards spiral. In these circumstances the process of restoring differentials for powerful worker groups becomes never ending.

Companies with a heavy investment in plant and machinery are particularly vulnerable. With a high ratio of capital to labour in the production process, line managers often feel inclined (if not justified) to buy peace at a cost which at first seems small and insignificant compared to the alternative of a shut-down. These pressures are compounded where a firm lacks any unused capacity (such a surplus is becoming increasingly rare in the current recession) and has competitors only too eager to 'snap up' disappointed customers. The automobile industry, the airlines and the chemicals industry have at times provided some examples of the type of problem under discussion here. Maintaining the production of automobiles has often taken precedence over dealing with deep-seated industrial relations problems; strikes in one firm can easily lead customers to examine the competition in other showroom windows, which windows are more likely to contain products from overseas. An airliner on the ground represents a massive dead charge on an airline's finances and needs to be kept in the air carrying revenue paying passengers for the maximum possible hours. Ground crews and maintenance staff have clearly appreciated their key position in an airline's operations, particularly since the advent of the jet age. Indeed some airlines possess very complex and bewildering remuneration structures which may well reflect the differential bargaining strengths of different employee groups. The chemicals firm manufacturing de-gradable products in expensive plant with finite storage capacity needs to continue production and distribution without interruptions. Its maintenance workers, drivers and despatch staff are in a position to exert considerable pressure in order to secure pecuniary advantage.

There may be some case for claiming that the influence of powerful bargaining groups in key operations has been the major cause of distortion and decay in remuneration structures. An important prerequisite to this claim must be the very structure of industrial relations in Britain. The large number of trade unions in many organizations means that there are more opportunities for groups to pressure management, and perhaps more importantly for other groups to join in the differential restoration or leapfrogging 'circuses'. Therefore, the problems created by collective bargaining pressures which lead to decay in remuneration structures, require solutions designed on a wider basis than a concern with pay alone. In the absence of such a development we can only resort to the claim that the management of industrial relations in general, and remuneration in particular, should be related to corporate needs and based on anticipative strategies which either avoid or better equip management to deal with *ad hoc* and short term pressures. With such a state of affairs the use of techniques such as job evaluation will have an opportunity to help develop improved pay structures.

Distortion and *ad hoc* change

A frequent and often depressing discovery in many organizations is the inability of managers to resist 'tinkering' with remuneration structures to achieve some short term gain. Usually such exercises are indulged in to overcome some small problem or grievance with the hope of 'buying off' the problem. Some employees and their shop steward representatives are very quick to identify some reason for raising a grievance on pay with which to pressure management and obtain some advantage. Changes in pay to allow for these limited issues represent a 'foot in the door' which leads to claims for comparability by other employees. The most obvious examples of reasons for these small scale changes are difficult working conditions: operating new equipment; operating equipment which is unique to a particular job or operation; work which involves occasional support to other operations and departments; work involving elements which are difficult to assess or measure such as hand and eye co-ordination or judgement; the age of an employee being above that of colleagues; recognition of above average length of service;

occasional requirements for operatives to fill in for absent supervision; introduction of incentive schemes; shift operations and new work practices; changes to the product and/or components; changes in type and use of tools; and finally, trying to convince an individual or group of employees that management really are willing to listen to and act upon employee views on what is fair and unfair. This list of reasons is incomplete, and readers will be aware of similar issues in their own organizations. Small scale changes may seem insignificant, harmless and right but can accumulate into awkward precedents which in turn can grow into major causes of dispute.

Implications

For management

It is relatively simple to suggest that management should resist any pressures to make *ad hoc* changes to remuneration structures in order to deal with what seems a small and limited problem. Many managers want to be seen to work in the interests of their subordinates, reward ability and achievement, bestow favours, and remove problems in order to keep production moving or to return to a more 'comfortable existence'. Changing the behaviour patterns of individual managers and their preferences requires more than a policy and strategy for management and more than management education and development. Management need to discover that it is more worthwhile to attempt the maintenance of the wage and salary structures than to indulge the claims of particular operatives. Such a situation can only exist if senior management back up middle and junior management in resisting pressure for *ad hoc* change. We may call this a particular management style, perhaps the style of strong management or purposive management; but such descriptions should be unnecessary. Management should naturally involve control and influence of elements of organizational life which are the prerequisites to the well-being of the organization; one such element is labour costs (and the remuneration structures which determine them). It is amazing how such control seems to escape management in so many organizations, and it is a constant concern of commentators and writers on the subject of remuneration. To deal with the problem a veritable consultancy and advisory industry has been built up around the problems of remuneration and reward in organizations.

For unions

The problems of irrational and decaying remuneration structures and the pressures giving rise to them, provide headaches for trade union representatives as much as for management. Indeed, many shop stewards known to the writer are more often than not reluctant to press home the grievances of their members but feel obliged to because the pay structure has become complex and characterized by precedents which they cannot ignore. If management would cease to set precedents, shop stewards and convenors would be much more effective in convincing employees of the sense of adhering to structures which have been determined by the normal processes of collective bargaining. Additionally, in some industries, such a situation would help full time officials convince shop stewards anxious to 'make their mark' of the wisdom of keeping to what has been previously agreed.

Management control

In the last analysis, the problem is management's. The pressures discussed in this chapter require a response from those who manage remuneration, and a response made with a regard to the longer term implications of decisions about remuneration structures. The perfection of these structures and the erasing of all problems and their causes is unlikely to be fully achieved mainly because of the very indeterminate nature of the social pressures which so often 'eat away' at effectiveness in wage and salary administration. For example, differences in the collective bargaining strengths of different employee groups will persist despite any attempts at rationality by management. But understanding the existence and the nature of these social pressures is a first step for management to take in learning how to cope with them more effectively, and learning which managerial responses to pressures and problems require improvement.

Effective wage and salary administration is facilitated by the clearing of obstacles to management control of labour costs. Such obstacles include shop floor restrictions on output, provision of special payments to cover down time, excessive overtime, lack of labour flexibility and impediments to managements' control of task allocations, employee abuse of time sheets by recording exaggerated levels of performance, loose performance standards for effort and/or output, weaknesses in supervisory management which cause many of the aforementioned problems and finally the very complexity of wage and salary structures. The means of eradicating these problems lies in the improvement of the quality of supervisory management, the backing of supervision by middle and senior management and the improvement of communications between these levels, improvements in the design and operation of incentive schemes and the simplification of remuneration structures. The redesign of remuneration structures will require techniques which will produce nothing on their own, but may contribute much if supported by an interventionist style of management.

Some organizations have gained from revision of the wage and salary structures involving the consolidation of all premium rates of pay and allowances into much simplified structures. The productivity agreements of the late sixties and early seventies provided numerous examples of how much scope for rationality existed in pay structures. The Alcan agreement provided for some 40 wage grades to be reduced to seven, while at Imperial Chemical Industries eight grades based on job evaluation were introduced to cover the whole of the adult male labour force.[8] An important benefit for the employee was increased stability of earnings from week to week or month to month and in some cases, wages and salaries have been determined and paid on an annual basis. This degree of stability can be a major pre-requisite to improved managerial control of remuneration because it removes many of the issues which cause anomalies and precedents, and thus disputes and decay. The importance and desirability of stabilized earnings within simplified remuneration structures lends some force to the argument that the trend to erase all premium payments and allowances which first started in the productivity agreements era of the 1960s (but disappeared in the 1970s) should be revived and brought to a satisfactory conclusion.

Job evaluation in the design of remuneration structures

In the attempt to put rationality and purpose into remuneration structures, job evaluation has proved attractive to many organizations. Methods of job evaluation have been in existence for more than half a century, but in the United Kingdom the popularity of this approach to designing pay structures has grown mainly during the past two to three decades. Usually, job evaluation is employed to achieve the following objectives:

(i)   To set a rate for the job irrespective of the attributes of individual employees

(ii) To determine the relationship between jobs and to establish a systematic structure for wage rates at the level of the firm. (This can also be achieved at industry and national level)

(iii) To determine, recognize and pay for the requirements of a job; for example, in terms of skill, education and degree of responsibility

(iv) To ensure that the resultant structure of pay levels meets both the organization's expectations and employee expectations.

There are several job evaluation methods or schemes available to help companies achieve these objectives and the choice will probably depend on the characteristics and particular problems facing the company.

Nature of job evaluation

Job evaluation involves the determination of the relative worth of jobs as a basis for the payment of differential wages and salaries. The assumptions behind job evaluation are consistent with a performance based remuneration policy and are as follows:

(i) That jobs contributing most to corporate objectives should receive the highest levels of remuneration

(ii) Therefore, that corporate performance is furthered by the results of job evaluation

(iii) The relative worth of jobs as a sound basis on which to achieve equity in payment systems.

It must be emphasized that worth can be measured in a variety of ways, depending on the type and complexity of the job evaluation scheme chosen.

The schemes available have traditionally been categorized under two headings; non-analytical and analytical. The former are simple methods which evaluate the worth of the job as a whole. The latter are more detailed, and employ factors identified in each job by means of job specifications which describe the degree to which the factors are present. It is these factors which give rise to the different measures of worth, and they can include skill, responsibility, education, working conditions, problem solving and effort.

In the sixties and seventies, several newer methods have emerged, which might be considered to form two more groups of schemes. The first groups include approaches which are designed to counter some of the weaknesses of the analytical and non-analytical methods. The Hay-MSL Guide Chart Profile and Direct Consensus Method belong to a group of job evaluation schemes which in this work are termed 'modern'. Finally, the fourth group includes the single factor methods such as Paterson's 'Decision Banding'.[9]

Which of the many schemes available will be chosen depends on the types of job to be evaluated, the number of jobs to be embraced, current pay structures, and the nature of collective bargaining and general characteristics of the firm. In other words the scheme chosen should be a function of, or contingent upon, those organizational characteristics which are deemed to be capable of influencing the job evaluation exercise, the outcome and the continuing maintenance of the results.

Whatever scheme is chosen, certain elements are common to all. In the first instance the idea of some kind of systematic evaluation for determining pay has to be acceptable to management and employees, and the pay differentials resulting from the evaluation exercise need to be similarly acceptable. Job descriptions of varying degrees of complexity and analysis, depending on the scheme used, are prepared to provide sufficient information on which to base an evaluation of the worth of jobs. These descriptions should be accurate, complete and acceptable to the holders. Members of an evaluating committee carry out the evaluations through their interpretation of the job descriptions under the guidance of a chairman. Some means should be devised to translate the results of the evaluations into financial values. Finally, those responsible for the job evaluation exercise should possess the skill, knowledge and experience to ensure accuracy in the job descriptions, fairness in the actual process of evaluation and pragmatism in the translation of job worth into money. This last point is merely to emphasize that the results of job evaluation will be judged, in the last analysis, on the degree to which they meet the expectations of the parties involved. The role of management in ensuring that such expectations are 'realistic' is considerable and dependent upon an appreciation of the realities of job evaluation as an aid to the management of remuneration and not a panacea for the ills of decaying remuneration structures.

Job evaluation is not a scientific means of determining pay. Rather it is an organized, rational, comparative and systematic approach to defining consistent relationships between pay for different jobs, which relationships are deemed to be equitable. In arriving at some degree of equity, the subjective evaluation of worth decreases in the attempt to increase the objective content of the process of evaluation through the use of job descriptions and a carefully selected and chaired evaluation committee.

Reasons for implementation

In the most extreme case, job evaluation is resorted to by organizations suffering from the types of pressures and problems discussed in this chapter, where pay structures have become so disordered and beyond management control that only a radical rebuilding of the differentials will contain decay and restore management control of remuneration. Less dramatically, it is interesting to note that in a comparatively recent publication, Incomes Data Services Ltd reveal 11 reasons for companies starting job evaluation and these are as follows:[10]

(i)   demands for a rational grading structure

(ii)   union recognition
(iii) moves to greater participation
(iv)   single status
(v)   sex discrimination and equal pay
(vi)   decay or disrepute of old systems
(vii) changes in technology and job content
(viii) relocation and mobility
(ix)   multinationals transferring staff between countries
(x)   allowing for future expansion
(xi)   changes in personnel staff.

Most if not all of these reasons will probably be familiar, but The Incomes Data Services publication reveals that 'demands for a rational grading structure' was the most frequently stated reason for the introduction of job evaluation.[11] It is also frequently the case that job evaluation schemes are introduced in an attempt to amend a previously installed scheme which has become out of date with the passage of time. Lupton and Bowey were of the opinion that *this* was the most common reason for installing job evaluation:

> It appears that most job evaluation schemes are introduced in order to replace old systems which had evolved from various unrelated past objectives with new systems based on current logically related values and aims.[12]

Quite often this exercise involves the replacement of a simple scheme with more complicated methods.

In the main there seems to be some consensus that job evaluation (whether fresh to the organization or familiar but of a newer type) is used to remove or ease the problems caused by pay differentials which have become confused and unrelated to current conditions and expectations. This is considered possible by the introduction of new differentials determined by some evaluation of job content on the basis of common or standard criteria.

In the list of reasons provided by Incomes Data Services Ltd, the issue of participation is noteworthy because in the vast majority of cases job evaluation is a joint exercise involving management and unions which provides the opportunity for greater understanding between the parties on the vital issue of pay. Single status refers to the problem of manual workers demanding the conditions applied to white-collar staffs. Adverse reaction by white-collar employees can be overcome by using job evaluation to establish and maintain the differentials. Mobility and transfers of staff can be facilitated if grading structures and the appropriate pay structures are standardized across the company. Such standardization can be facilitated by job evaluation. If a flexible form of job evaluation is used (*see* the next section) the way is cleared for new jobs to be quickly slotted into the grades in times of expansion. Finally, newly appointed personnel managers may attempt to introduce a job evaluation scheme to achieve more readily understood remuneration structures, or perhaps to 'make their mark' on the organization.

Whatever the reason for introducing a job evaluation scheme to the organization, the result should be a hierarchy of jobs which may be broken down into grades. With the exception of two, little used, schemes in Britain, job evaluation does not directly determine the level or rate of pay. That rate may be determined by factors beyond the influence of job evaluation such as collective bargaining and conditions in the labour market.

Conditions unsuitable for job evaluation

If management are unclear about the nature of the pressures which influence remuneration levels then the results of job evaluation will soon be destroyed. Such pressures will not go away because a new set of pay differentials has been established. Therefore management understanding of factors influencing pay coupled with anticipation of results and the means to control remuneration in the face of complex influences is a pre-requisite to the successful application of job evaluation. The structures derived from the evaluation exercise should not be considered 'sacred' at the expense of adjusting to reality and change, otherwise events will make the structures look less rational and equitable than they did on introduction. Thus the abilities of management to handle the results of job evaluation over time will be a determinant of the long term success of job evaluation. The management of any flexibility in the differentials following the initial evaluation exercise will inevitably require responses to problems which are an improvement on those which caused the difficult remuneration structures now considered in need of replacement. Consultants and advisers in particular are in a position to recognize whether or not management are able to succeed with job evaluation and can thus advise appropriately on how the client can improve management capabilities to cope more effectively.

Changes
Changes in technology of production and product, in labour market pay differentials, in attitudes and expectations and in trade union power create substantial difficulties for job evaluation. In this context, it is not

only management ability which is of concern; the ability of many methods of job evaluation to cope with change and uncertainty is limited. A few methods do offer some flexibility, particularly such modern methods as profiling and direct consensus (*see* pages 87–92). But in the main, these cover changes in job content arising from developments within production processes. The problems of the labour market, attitudes and collective bargaining are rather more intractable. A frequent response to the presence of these problems is some regular audit of the pay levels through the reapplication of the evaluation scheme. It is sometimes difficult for employees to determine any difference between this re-evaluation and the kind of 'fiddling' with rates which was discussed earlier. Certainly the claims for rationality and equity in the original job evaluation exercise will soon appear false if management demonstrate that the evaluated structures are adaptable and negotiable in the face of union pressure. Any adjustment to pay levels may lead the way to increasing demands from employees to move rates of pay in line with changing conditions in the organization and in the labour market. Reference to this problem can be found in the section on points rating in the context of 'grade drift' in the following chapter.

Comparability

These problems raise the issue of external consistency and the notion of some desired relationship between the organization's remuneration structure and those obtaining in the community. It is this external comparability which creates the main difficulty for job evaluation. But this should not mean that job evaluation, collective bargaining and labour market developments are incompatible. Job evaluation can be seen as dealing with internal consistency in pay differentials while collective bargaining deals with external consistency of the organization's total remuneration structure. The nub of the problem is the multi-union structure of many organizations which works against any overall uniformity within the remuneration structure and 'eats away' at the consistency in differentials. The relative strengths of different unions in particular sometimes present unanswerable questions to the proponents of job evaluation. We may conclude, therefore, that the effective management of industrial relations is a necessary pre-requisite to the successful maintenance of the outcomes of job evaluation.

Costs

Costs associated with job evaluation should be a determinant of the decision to proceed with a scheme. Normally the more complicated the method the greater the cost. Additionally, the introduction of the new pay structures will usually be accompanied by an 'across the board' pay increase to enhance acceptability to the labour force thus pushing up costs further. So the scheme adopted must be cost effective and absorb design, installation and maintenance costs and a pay increase. If these costs cannot be contained it may be appropriate for management to turn aside from job evaluation and consider the continued use of informal procedures. Even in cases where the evaluation exercise can be justified in financial terms, care will still be needed in the choice of scheme if long term costs are to be acceptable and the time and effort needed by job evaluation is not to exceed the capacity of the organization.

The number of jobs

The number of jobs to be evaluated should also be a determinant of whether to adopt job evaluation and will influence the type of scheme chosen. There are no hard and fast rules on the minimum number of jobs necessary to justify job evaluation, but a number less than 100 may be adequately structured by means of some simple form of grading. Nonetheless, this writer has seen examples of job evaluation schemes applied to as few as 25 jobs, and the use of consultants on exercises involving 40 to 80 jobs. In the majority of these cases, the methods used were simple and the costs were acceptable to management because new pay differentials were the means to clearing away obstacles to the introduction of new production processes, changed working practices and demanning. In some instances the job evaluation was used to 'buy out' overtime and shift payments (in the case of manual workers) and merit rating schemes (for white-collar and technical and administrative staffs).

With more than 100 jobs, the evaluation scheme chosen will probably need to be quite sophisticated, and the use of consultants may be necessary. As the spread of jobs to be covered increases, the more likely will be the demands for a detailed appreciation of how grades have been determined and the more simple types of evaluation will be short of adequate information and analysis to answer the questions satisfactorily.

As a 'rule of thumb' guide we may conclude that less than 50 jobs may be dealt with through simple adjustment of grades by the personnel department, 50 to 100 jobs may be effectively graded through a simple non-analytical method carried out by the personnel department and more than 100 jobs will require a complex and analytical method perhaps involving the use of outside consultants depending on the resources available to the organization's personnel function.

Job categories

Job categories sometimes create confusion in terms of which jobs are suitable for job evaluation. Some people seem to think that job evaluation is only suitable for white collar groups while others see it as appropriate to manual grades. Just why this confusion has arisen is not clear, but it represents a problem often encountered by this writer in discussions with managers, trade union officials and employees. In some instances, job evaluation has been seen as being for white-collar workers, what incentive schemes have been to the shop floor. In fact job evaluation is suitable for all jobs, although different schemes may be necessary to deal with different groups. Comprehensive schemes which attempt to embrace all types of job tend to encounter difficulty in applying the same criteria to evaluate say the work of a sheet metal worker and the work of a research and development manager. Clearly qualifications, responsibility, working conditions and decision making are going to be very different in these two jobs and limited in providing a basis for comparability.

Expectations

Job evaluation should not be introduced to serve as a vehicle for accepting trade union demands on pay which are rightly the subject for collective bargaining. Schemes should be introduced as genuine and jointly agreed methods of restructuring remuneration in the interests of rationality, control and equity. In this connection, it is worth adding that it is by no means unknown for consultants and personnel managers to commence a job evaluation exercise only to realize that managerial and union expectations for the scheme are no more than some justification for the continuation of the present differentials and their inherent anomalies. Management and unions share the responsibility for dealing with such expectations and for ensuring that the results of job evaluation enjoy the benefit of a positive climate within an organization which allows adequate opportunity for new differentials to be applied and maintained.

Conclusions

The problems of irrationality in remuneration structures are basically tied up with the issues of complexity and differentials. Pay for similar work, pay for similar levels of effort, and differences in pay for different levels of responsibility are some of the areas where employees come to feel that pay is not wholly fair or equitable. Building in some degree of fairness is a major element in effective remuneration structure design and can underpin effective management of pay. This fairness cannot provide 'perfection' in structure; it provides some degree of compromise between the need for perfection and the need to recognize the social realities and expectations within the organization. Job evaluation can be used to provide this 'workable' compromise provided it is accompanied by the application of management skill and judgement in dealing with social factors (and indeed other indeterminate pressures in the environment) in the interests of corporate need. This aware and interventionist style of management is the first requirement for the containment of any deterioration in pay structures and a pre-requisite for the profitable use of the job evaluation methods discussed in the following chapter.

References

1   INCOMES DATA SERVICES LTD *Cutting the working week*, Study 264, April 1982. Also, *Implementing a shorter working week*, Study 244, Nov 1981. Also see, 'Overtime: restricting its level' in *Industrial Relations Review and Report* No 270, April 1982, pp 2–8.

2   CARBY K *and* EDWARDS-STUART F, *The overtime dilemma*, Institute of Personnel Management, 1981.

3   SMITH I G, *The measurement of productivity*, Gower Press 1974.

4   INCOMES DATA SERVICES LTD Report 365, November 1981, p 23.

5   See INSTITUTE OF MANPOWER STUDIES, *Work sharing potential – an examination of selected firms*, 1981.

6   NATIONAL BOARD FOR PRICES AND INCOMES Report No 65, *Payment by results systems*, Cmnd 3627, HMSO 1968, para 34.

7   LUPTON T *and* BOWEY A M, *Wages and salaries*. Penguin 1974. chapter 2.

8   SMITH I G *Loc cit.*

9   PATERSON T, *Job evaluation*, Business Books 1972.

10 INCOMES DATA SERVICES LTD, *Guide to job evaluation*. March 1979, p 1.

11 *Ibid.*

12 LUPTON T *and* BOWEY A M, *Wages and salaries*. Penguin 1974 p 20.

4
Methods of job evaluation

A large number of job evaluation schemes are currently available and each may be appropriate to particular organizational conditions. The present chapter provides an assessment of these schemes and discusses their application. Additionally, elements of procedure are discussed to guide the reader in the effective application of job evaluation as a means to underpin the design of sound payment structures and the effective management of remuneration.

Preparing the ground

Assuming that the problems and conditions discussed in chapter 3 do not impinge on the organization, or do so but can be managed effectively, an initial decision to proceed with job evaluation for a particular range of jobs can be made and should be followed by a series of decisions about any problems which will need special attention. This will involve consideration of legal requirements on the issue of equal pay future changes (such as technology) which are likely to influence the results of job evaluation, and the relationship of the exercise (or rather the results in terms of new pay differentials) to collective bargaining arrangements and the present grade structures.

The problem of sex equality is particularly interesting since many evaluation exercises hinge on the masculine type of job requirement such as physical effort. A conscious decision to give adequate attention to an appropriate spread of elements or factors in work, and the inclusion of women in the evaluation team to provide equality in the evaluation of jobs for females and males, is very often an essential 'early step'.

The effect of changes within the organization, particularly in technology, requires some 'forecasting of events' in order to determine an appropriately designed evaluation scheme which can embrace new jobs and changed job content. A guide here is an examination of past influences on previous remuneration structures.

The issues for collective bargaining, which are raised by the introduction of job evaluation, include the problem of several unions being required to accept a standard remuneration structure and the question of employee representation on the evaluation committee (refer to page 99 for a discussion on the composition of the committee). It is normal for unions to have representation on the committee, but difficulties can arise on deciding whether shop stewards or other employees should be brought into the exercise. Certainly the people whose jobs are to be evaluated should be represented, and the advantage of this arrangement is that resultant gradings are jointly determined, thus ensuring a degree of employee commitment to the results of job evaluation. Full consultations with shop floor representatives should characterize every step in the procedure.

An appropriate time scale should be determined for the job evaluation exercise and a decision taken on whether to use consultants. It is normal for job evaluation exercises to take a minimum of six months, and managements and union representatives should allow for this if they are aiming for completion on some particular annual settlement date. One of the major time consuming elements is the preparation of job descriptions, which almost inevitably causes slippage in the programme. A preliminary trial run of the scheme, or pilot study, may also be pursued to provide some familiarity in evaluating and recognizing problems.

Consultants can bring several advantages to the application of job evaluation. They can save management time, provide an outside and objective view of the evaluation, give specialist knowledge and expertise, and an independence which may help acceptance of the scheme by employees. They may be able to provide training and education in job evaluation for company managers and employees, and an 'in house' scheme supported by an auditing system to maintain the grades over time, although the choice of such a scheme requires some consideration. 'In house' schemes may not suit all organizations, although many consultancy companies have now prepared much more flexible methods which allow for more intervention, and therefore greater understanding and control by the client. Despite the additional costs incurred in the use of consultants, their services on job evaluation seem to be attractive in many cases.

With decisions made on the issues discussed above, the job evaluation exercise can be started, and attention can now turn to an assessment of the choice of methods currently available.

Traditional schemes

Non-analytical schemes

The three non-analytical schemes are RANKING, CLASSIFICATION or GRADING, and PAIRED COMPARISONS.

Ranking

Ranking is the simplest scheme with evaluation sometimes being based on job titles only, although job descriptions are preferable. The evaluation committee ranks benchmark or key jobs in order of worth to represent the top, bottom and mid-points of the range which in turn provides a guide for the evaluation of the remaining jobs which are slotted in around these benchmarks. Finally, the ranked jobs are divided into grades which have salary ranges or brackets attached to them. An important feature of the evaluation process is the comparison of job against job in determining worth or importance to the company.

The ranking method can be workable for exercises involving up to 50 jobs, and the system is easy to understand, design and install. On the debit side this scheme provides no measure of the difference between jobs and is not totally impersonal because the evaluation committee reach decisions on the basis of opinion rather than some logical and rational approach to a detailed assessment of the job. This reliance on opinion can bias the results because the job-holder rather than the job may be considered, and the problem increases where the spread of jobs exceeds the spread of knowledge held by the committee members.

Grading or classification

Grading or classification also treats the whole job, but in this case the grades are determined first and these grades become the means of measuring job worth. Consequently, the grades can be deemed to represent a scale of values for worth or importance to the company. Grade descriptions are prepared first and the evaluation committee slots each job into an appropriate grade by comparing these descriptions with the whole job. This type of scheme has proved popular in the public sector and in organizations with a high proportion of clerical staff. The National Coal Board and Civil Service have been major users of grading or classification. The Institute of Administrative Management have developed their own grading or classification scheme.

Grading shares with ranking the advantages of ease of implementation and operation. The scheme is readily understood, is inexpensive and quick to introduce and can be applied to a small number of jobs. Unlike ranking, the grading approach provides some measure of worth in the form of the grade descriptions or definitions, although this is a dubious advantage if the grades coincide with a predetermined salary structure (as can often be the case) because the knowledge of money values may bias the evaluations. Furthermore, grading is only suitable for simple jobs which readily fit into the grades. More complex jobs may be spread across more than one grade. For example, clerical officer, section leader and supervisor may be so sufficiently similar in terms of job requirements that in the classification scheme they will be covered by the one general grade description, a situation often leading to dispute between the holders of such jobs and management. Grade descriptions are relevant to one type of job only; so for example, clerical schemes fall down in application to manual jobs and even fail to cope with categories nearer home such as managerial, administrative and technical occupations. Finally, this type of scheme depends on fixed grades which may allow for no up-date in response to changes in job content over time.

Paired comparisons
Paired comparisons represents a development of the ranking method, and also forms a basis for the modern method of direct consensus. Again the whole job is considered and the evaluation process involves comparing each job with every other job, in turn. To facilitate the exercise a score chart is necessary and as the job is compared with the others it scores 2 points if its worth is considered greater than the worth of the other job, 1 point if of equal worth, and no points when considered to be of less worth. When the job comparisons are completed, the points score can be totalled. At the conclusion of the complete exercise all jobs have a total score which allows them to be ranked. The assignment of scores may look something like the following simple example.

Job	Comparative scores				Total score	Rank order
	A	B	C	D		
A	–	0	2	0	2	3
B	2	–	1	1	4	2
C	0	1	–	0	1	4
D	2	1	2	–	5	1

Paired comparisons shares many of the advantages of the two other non-analytical schemes and in particular is easy to understand, quick to implement and inexpensive. On the other hand there is still no real analysis of why there are differences between jobs. Additionally, the fact that job D scores three points more than job A may bear no resemblance to the actual differences between D and A. One final point is the need for computer back up, as the number of jobs increases in the comparisons exercise (100 jobs will require 2,450 recorded comparisons).

A summary note on non-analytical schemes

Despite the considerable disadvantages attaching to non-analytical schemes, their popularity cannot be denied. We may conclude that they have some use in producing a hierarchy of jobs in a situation where resources are limited, job numbers are small and control of the actual evaluation exercise is effective. Additionally, ranking in particular can be a quick means to checking on the results obtained by using a more complex method. In this way the evaluation committee can assess the degree of 'felt fairness' in the positioning of jobs. Assuming that simplicity is not the only criteria for choosing a scheme, the evidence suggests that the organization might benefit from considering a more sophisticated type of scheme, if resources permit.

Analytical methods

This grouping includes the points rating and factor comparison methods which involve a more detailed and analytical approach to the evaluation of job worth. This approach is facilitated by concentrating on elements or factors which it is considered are common to all jobs yet differentially affect their relative worth. It is important to emphasize that the factors used in these schemes must exist in all jobs to be reviewed.

Points rating

Points rating has become very popular and normally embraces such factors as skill, effort, responsibility, decision making, working conditions, contacts with other people and education. Such factors will require qualification; for example, what type of skill is required and what is the nature of the responsibility? The actual number of factors to be used will depend on particular organizational conditions and may vary from a minimum of four (skill, responsibility, effort and working conditions are normally chosen) to as many as 15 or more depending on the degree of 'fine tuning' or qualifications required. One scheme in the United States employs factors as follows:[1]

Sill in terms of:	Responsibility for:	Effort:	Working conditions:
1 Education	4 Equipment or process	8 Mental and visual	10 Normal
2 Experience	5 Material or product	9 Physical	11 Hazardous
3 Initiative and ingenuity	6 Safety of others		
	7 Work of others		

No matter how many factors are chosen, the results tend to be the same whether a few or many are used. In the last analysis, management and employee representatives should decide which and how many to use. In particular, the views of employees should be taken into account. They have a clear understanding of job requirements and will be ultimately responsible for sanctioning the introduction of the scheme. A minimum of four and maximum of seven factors is sufficient for most organizations' requirements.

Values: With the factors chosen and clearly defined each is allocated a range of points. For example, if the factor of education is included in the scheme it may be allocated a range of points to a total of 180 as follows:

1 Proficiency required in written English and Arithmetic—20 points.

2 Five years of secondary school to CSE (2 passes)—40 points.

3 Five years of secondary school to GCE 'O' Level (2 passes)—60 points.

4 Seven years of secondary education to GCE 'A' Level (1 pass)—80 points.

5 Attendance at technical college with Higher National Diploma— 100 points.

NB the above is only an example and is not intended to be representative of any scheme or any actual evaluation of educational qualifications.

Weighting: The factors are weighted so that those which are of the most importance to the organization obtain the highest scores. This weighting can be achieved by using percentages so that skill may account for 30 per cent, education for 20 per cent, effort for 15 per cent, working conditions for 25 per cent, and responsibility for 10 per cent. These percentages can be used as a multiplier in calculating the total

82

points score in each job. Alternatively, weighting can be determined by allocating different points totals to factors, so education may have a maximum of 100 points, while effort may only have 80 points and working conditions 60 points maximum. Thus the range of points for effort (physical) may be as follows, and can be compared with education above:

1 No significant amount of effort required—20 points.
2 Frequent handling of objects less than 5 lb in weight—40 points.
3 Repetitive and occasionally sustained handling of objects between 5 and 20 lb in weight—60 points.
4 Manual work with frequent physical strain and lifting objects over 20 lb in weight—80 points.

The described requirements 1, 2, 3 and 4 for effort are termed degrees or levels of the factor, and it is the degree of a factor which the evaluator is looking for in each job. It should also be noted that even though a factor may not actually appear in a job, it still obtains a points score (for example, no significant amount of effort scores 20). It is an insult to a job-holder to score zero.

The process of determining the points, weightings and degrees is essentially arbitrary, and decisions must be taken as to how much, in terms of points, one degree is worth more or less than another and one factor is worth more or less, in terms of weighting than another. Furthermore, such decisions are made more complicated because it must be determined if, say, 'GCE 'A' level passes' are worth more or less points than 'frequent physical strain'.

In the last analysis, the number of points assigned to factors may be considered an irrelevance because the weightings actually do the job of maintaining the relative importance of the factors. In the examples given above the points are in multiples of 10; they could just as readily be in multiples of 15, 20, 50 or 100. But in choosing the points scores it should be remembered that it is easier to justify not raising a job (and therefore the person in it) to a higher grade if it is 20 points below 500 and not 1 point below 50. As with choice of factors, the organization will choose the points, weightings and degrees which can be 'lived with' by the parties concerned.

Procedure: the procedure used in points rating is based on job descriptions which contain enough analysis of the job to allow for an appreciation of the degree or level to which each factor is present and for some comparison with the pre-determined definitions for the factor degrees. With such a comparison exercise, the evaluators can then determine the degree level for each factor in each job. At the end of the exercise all jobs will have a total points score which can be divided into grades based on point ranges. Usually, the grades are a result of plotting the job scores against salaries in the form of a scatter diagram or 'scattergram'.

NB The above discussion of the points rating system simplifies what is a multi-step, and sometimes involved, approach to determining levels of remuneration. The reader is referred to chapter 5 for a detailed appreciation of wage and salary determination by job evaluation.

Advantages: Perhaps the first advantage to be considered in connection with points rating is its avoidance of the over-simplification inherent in non-analytical schemes. In the analysis of factors, any bias which can come about by evaluating whole jobs (and thus the job holder) gives way to the greater objectivity which job evaluation schemes should be pursuing anyway. Because the use of factors is at the heart of the scheme, points rating can be applied to all categories of jobs by using different factor definitions and/or combinations of factors. Once a remuneration structure has been established by this type of scheme, it is a simple matter to introduce new jobs by evaluation against the various factors rather than against the whole range of jobs. The degree of analysis contained in the points rating approach has been seen to give strong justification to its acceptance by managements and trade unions. Trade unions have also gained in terms of being able to negotiate on factors as well as pay. In discussing job evaluation with trade unionists, and particularly in teaching the subject on TUC courses for shop stewards, this writer has been impressed with their knowledge of the subject and their preference for the points rating method. This is perhaps, as the TUC has stated, because this approach '. . . causes people to look more closely at the elements that make up a job and helps to identify anomalies, distortions and injustices in wage rates.'[2] The remuneration structures deriving from points rating schemes have proved to be durable over time, but doubts about the inflexibility of such structures of the incomes policies and inflation emerged during the late 1970s.

Disadvantages: Incomes polices limit pay increases and therefore employees seek to achieve their aspirations through appeals against the grading of their jobs, claiming that factors such as responsibility or effort or skill have increased. If 'management' accommodate such pressures they will allow higher scoring for such factors. When this occurs employees and shop stewards sense that such scores are given to the high weighted factors; that is, those deemed to be the most important to the organization. Thus jobs can 'drift' up the grades, and such drifting has become the 'achilles heel' of points rating schemes. A cure for this problem can be found in limiting the number of degrees or levels for each factor and the points assigned to them. In this connection, it is worth noting that low weighted factors with limited points ranges are the most stable over time. However, there is increasing evidence that grade drift is being tackled by the introduction of increased flexibility in modern methods of job evaluation which are a development of points rating, and which are discussed in the next section.

One disadvantage traditionally raised in connection with points rating is complexity in design, installation and maintenance and the associated problems of cost and difficulty in understanding. It is trite to argue that complex problems cannot be solved by simplistic solutions, but organizations should carefully consider the disadvantages of the simple non-analytical schemes against the advantages of the more sophisticated schemes. Nonetheless, the time and resources needed for the points rating type of scheme are considerable, and may require the full time attention of someone skilled in job evaluation.

The use of factors, weightings and numerical measures gives an 'illusion' of precision in the points rating process. In fact opinion characterizes every step: factors, weightings, degrees and points, and the evaluations are judgements. At times factors can be defined in a most generalized way (*see* the examples given earlier in this section) and much discussion and negotiation can centre on factors and weightings. Outright argument is not unknown because employee representatives question the validity of measuring different factors on the same scale of values.

Summary: Despite these disadvantages, points rating does attempt to get to grips with an analysis of jobs divorced from any implications for remuneration. Until salary ranges are determined, the job itself is the centre of attention in an exercise which can provide a significant degree of objectivity. It is applicable to all job categories and many organizations have found it a suitable means for restoring some equity and rationality to remuneration structures.

Factor comparison

Factor comparison is an analytical scheme little used in Britain. Five factors only are used and they are mental effort, skill, physical effort, responsibility and working conditions. It is claimed that this limitation to five factors reduces the risk of double counting inherent in points rating schemes which sometimes use so many factors that they tend to overlap one another. In the United States, where the scheme was developed, factor comparison has been claimed to be suitable to manual jobs, although evidence is difficult to find on this side of the Atlantic. The most unfortunate feature of the method, however, must be the fact that evaluation is in monetary values; something which can give rise to bias.

There are four main steps involved in factor comparison:

(i)   key jobs are selected which are considered to be representative of the wage or salary levels
(ii) these jobs are analysed to determine what proportions of the total wage are paid for each factor
(iii) scales are established for each factor so that all other jobs can be compared factor by factor to arrive at a ranking for the range of jobs
(iv) with the exercise carried out in money values a straight calculation of cash value by factor provides the rate for all jobs under review.

Two major problems colour any assessment of factor comparison. By relating pay to the rank order of the job, negotiation of pay is brought into the evaluation exercise, something which is anathema to the trade unions in this country. The factors are determinants of total pay and do not allow for shift payments, overtime and bonus payments which would distort the money values established by the evaluation committee. In this last connection factor comparison seems more suitable to the consolidated pay, bereft of premium payments, more usually found on the other side of the Atlantic.

A summary note on analytical schemes

Points rating is clearly the analytical scheme worthy of consideration. It has been attractive to many organizations despite any limitations, and has provided a basis for several modern schemes. Indeed, these latter schemes are giving new life to points rating.

Modern schemes

These are sometimes called 'proprietary brands' because many have been developed by consultancy companies and academics, to avoid the limitations experienced with the more traditional methods discussed above. Several of these schemes are developments of points rating and are worthy of attention by organizations willing to cope with the costs and complexity in order to enhance the gains accruing from a more sophisticated approach to job evaluation. Other methods represent rather more radical attempts to improve job evaluation. Six methods are considered here and fall under three headings which are profiling, paired comparisons and single factor schemes.

Profiling

The two schemes in this grouping are the guide chart profiles developed by Hay-MSL and the profile method from Urwick, Orr and Partners. The reader will notice the presence of points rating and ranking in the following discussion.

Guide chart profiles

Guide Chart Profiles have become extremely popular for managerial, clerical and administrative staffs, although they are virtually ignored for manual job categories. In recent years, however, there has been evidence that the scheme's range of applications has been growing. There are three key elements to the scheme:

(i) jobs are evaluated on the basis of factors as in a points rating approach
(ii) ranking or profiling is used to check the rank order of the evaluation results
(iii) the scores for the jobs are directly plotted against a salary structure which is determined by a survey of salaries paid for comparable jobs in other employing organizations in the labour market. This last element has proved an attractive feature of the Guide Chart Profile and provides a response to the frequently raised criticism of job evaluation that results fail to reflect labour market realities:

Three factors are used: problem solving, know-how and account-ability. Whether prospective client organizations will accept that the intellectual act of problem solving, the detailed knowledge (know-how) underpinning decisions and the responsibility or accountability for taking decisions exist in all jobs to be reviewed is open to speculation. The factors are broken down into sub-factors:

(i) Problem solving includes constraints imposed by the organiza-tion and the degree to which thinking is restricted or free (the thinking environment sub-factor). Also, the nature of the intellectual exercise, whether routine or creative, is taken into account (the thinking challenge sub-factor)

(ii) Know-how is broken down into three groups of sub-factors: Skill, education and training; breadth of managerial know-how (including planning, organization and control); and human relations skills

(iii) Accountability embraces two sub-factors. Freedom to act and scope or magnitude of the accountability.

Procedure: As with a points rating scheme, each sub-factor is assigned a number of degree levels with points scores. Weightings are determined to reflect relative importance to the organization. The degree scores make up into a matrix which forms the basis of guide charts for each factor. These guide charts are guide lines with which the evaluation committee can assess the jobs to be reviewed. The degree to which each factor exists in the jobs is thus determined to provide job profiles.

Within the actual evaluation exercise, 'steps' are determined between jobs to provide a measure of difference. The evaluation committee defines one step for a noticeable difference, two steps for a clear difference and so on. Each step is awarded a percentage value, 10, 15 or 20 per cent being normal. In this way problem solving, know-how and accountability are formed into some sort of relationship within each job to produce the job profiles. But the exercise is not yet complete. The traditional method of ranking is now used to check the fairness and acceptability of the profiles. This is followed by the determination of the final rank order of jobs in relation to pay levels by plotting a scatter diagram or 'scattergram'.

It is at this stage that labour market information on rates of pay come into use. This information is obtained from the Hay-MSL annual salary surveys and allows comparison to be made between the salaries plotted within the client organization and those paid within other organizations using the scheme. In this way the client can see the relative position of salaries compared with those paid elsewhere and thus more effectively and assuredly decide whether or not to move towards comparability with the trend in market rates.

Advantages: The guide chart profile method is not so much a job evaluation scheme as a labour market survey coupled to job evaluation. It is popular, well proven and thorough in its approach to pay determination. It also helps to alleviate some of the apprehension about the 'realism' and 'competitiveness' of the results by conducting the salary survey among other organizations using the scheme. The analysis provided by points rating is linked to a process of verification in the form of ranking, and the use of sub-factors has improved flexibility in terms of the scheme's application to various categories of white-collar jobs.

Disadvantages: Overtime, guide chart profiling requires an audit to counter the problem of grade drift (discussed in connection with points rating earlier). Hay-MSL normally provide such services on an annual basis. The scheme represents a package, and as such may be pre-determined with few design features tailor-made to the clients' circumstances. Only companies using the method are included in the salary survey and therefore the results of that survey may be limited.

Finally, the guide chart profile method breaks with the tradition of job evaluation to evaluate the job and not the holder. In analysing accountability, know-how and problem solving, the evaluation exercise is by definition 'drawing in' the attributes which the individual brings to the job. Problem solving, know-how and accountability can be very personal factors and dependent on the individual. This may cause bias in the results unless the evaluation exercise is carefully and closely controlled.

The profile method

The Profile Method is associated with Urwick, Orr and Partners and is again a combination of points rating and ranking methods. Six factors are normally chosen: responsibility, knowledge, mental demands, social demands, physical demands and working conditions. Each factor is broken down into twelve characteristics and levels or 'degrees' are determined for these characteristics. But only four levels are defined: basic, moderate, high and exceptional.

Procedure: The work of the evaluation committee is to determine the levels at which the factor characteristics are present in the jobs under review. In this way each job is given a 'profile'. Bench mark or key jobs are evaluated and provided with profiles first, so that the committee can agree clear definitions for the four levels in each factor characteristic. By the use of straight job ranking or paired comparisons the jobs are placed into a rank order (see the section on ranking and paired comparisons earlier in this chapter) and a computer programme for regression analysis is used to provide a 'best fit' between the profiles derived from the 'key-job' evaluation and the rank order derived from the ranking or paired comparisons. In other words, two evaluations are used: a points rating to provide an analytical base to the factor profiles in the jobs, and ranking (paired comparisons) to provide a rank order which is felt to be fair by the committee.

The computer programme 'best fit' provides weightings for the factors which should reflect the organizations requirements. These weights are the amounts by which the factor scores for basic or moderate or high or exceptional should be multiplied in order to produce rank orders for the jobs.

To recap, factors and their weightings are determined through the results of points rating and paired comparisons applied to key jobs. A computer program converts these results into weights, the factor scores are then 'weighted' through multiplication by the computer determined weightings.

The remaining jobs are evaluated by comparison with the factor scores for bench mark jobs. The factor weightings are used to provide weighted profiles and total points scores for each job calculated. When all jobs have been profiled, they are grouped together in grades and through the plotting of a scatter diagram, the appropriate remuneration scales are applied as in a points rating scheme.

Summary
The overall complexity and structuring of the profile methods may at first appear a disadvantage, but in fact it provides simplified evaluation coupled with the advantages of an analytical scheme. In the use of four levels of assessment for each factor, the committee's job is simplified and the factor weightings are less dependent on opinion because of the introduction of computer analysis to measure the results of two evaluation exercises. All categories of jobs can be effectively treated by profiling, although factors do tend to be different between manual and white collar categories. Four levels of scoring not only ensures simplicity, but reduces debate among the members of the evaluation committee. More importantly, it ensures consistency in the scoring. Even overtime, as new jobs are added or existing jobs reviewed, the grade structures are less prone to drift than with points rating schemes and the requirement for maintenance of the structures is consequently reduced. Reviews are still required, however, to maintain the profiles as originally determined.

The use of a 'felt-fair' check on the profiles through ranking or paired comparisons involves employees closely in the evaluation exercise. Such participation has been held up as an advantage for the profile method. The advancement of the participative process in any job evaluation is to be warmly recommended.

In using the profile method the same warning that attaches to analytical methods must be heeded. Care must be taken in the choice of factors to ensure that they are appropriate to the organizations' conditions, the nature of the jobs and do not overlap or duplicate job requirements.

Paired comparisons

One method is considered under this heading. Its aim is to maximize consensus among the members of the evaluation committee coupled with precision through the use of a computer program for regression analysis—a very popular combination for modern job evaluation methods. The scheme is available in both simple and complex forms.

The direct consensus method

The direct consensus method is based on paired comparisons (see the section earlier in this chapter). The members of the evaluation committee compare key or bench mark jobs with the aid of job descriptions in order to choose which of each pair is the more important to the organization. This exercise is carried out in isolation by each committee member to avoid debate, and the results are fed into a computer program which in turn produces a rank order for the bench mark jobs. This rank order reveals the degree of consensus and disagreement among the committee members. Any disagreement on the worth of jobs is dealt with by the evaluation committee. The committee then slots in remaining jobs around the bench mark rankings and also agrees the grading structure for all jobs. Remuneration rates for the structure can be determined by reference to market rates or collective bargaining or company policy.

The direct consensus method (DCM) is readily understood, quick and inexpensive to install, and applicable to all employee categories. It involves a great deal of participation for employee representatives in the evaluation exercise and agreement on the results of the scheme is assured from a very early stage. Only the evaluation results are considered for the grading, and monetary values can be dealt with by the appropriate processes within the organization.

On the debit side, a consensus in the original evaluation exercise may not survive over time to deal with new or disputed jobs. There is no analysis of the jobs to justify differences in their worth. These deficiencies may be dealt with by the introduction of factors to the DCM approach, which development also makes DCM appropriate to job numbers in excess of 50.

The direct consensus factor method

The direct consensus factor method retains the advantages of the DCM approach while reducing the level of subjectivity in the job comparisons

91

by introducing job analysis on the basis of factors. Five factors are normally chosen and typically may be: responsibility, experience and training, physical requirements, supervision (given or required) and working conditions.

In the early stages the factor method follows the normal DCM procedure and involves the preparation of job descriptions, the selection of bench mark jobs, the preparation of a rank order for these sample jobs and the determination of grades for this rank order. The process does not stop here however, and the next stage is the choosing of factors. With the factors chosen, the members of the evaluation committee use the paired comparison method to evaluate each key job factor by factor, a task which is completed in isolation. As with DCM, the committee then meet to discuss any job for which there is no concensus and determine a definitive rank order for the key jobs. A computer program takes the overall rank order and the job factor rank order to produce weighting for each factor, usually expressed in points. The remaining jobs are then evaluated by the points rating method, placed in rank order and the grades determined.

A major advantage of the factor method for direct concensus is that the computer provides a measure of concensus and disagreement, identifies problem jobs and speeds up the evaluation process. As with the simpler non-factor based approach, the method is readily understood, quick to implement, inexpensive, and retains a high level of participation. The use of factors increases objectivity and the scheme has been applied with equal success in a wide range of industries and across a wide range of jobs.

Single factor schemes

The more traditional forms of job evaluation, non-analytical and analytical schemes, have often failed to maintain consistency of evaluation results over time. New jobs and changes in job content have frequently been inadequately accommodated, resulting in disputes and 'grade drift'. Furthermore many schemes are appropriate for one or a limited number of employee categories only. Single factors schemes represent a real attempt to deal with such problems by using only one factor in the evaluation exercise.

Time-span method

Time-span method is based on the time-span of discretion theory developed by Professor Elliot Jacques on the basis of his research work in the Glacier Metal Company.[3] In order to overcome the subjectivity of job evaluation schemes, he identifies two dimensions in work:

prescribed and discretionary elements. The prescribed element involves supervision of the worker and the discretionary element involves the workers' freedom to exercise responsibility, make decisions and initiate actions without any recourse to the supervisor. This discretionary element is the single factor which Jacques seeks to measure. He claims that it can be measured in terms of the span of time in which the employee is left to exercise his own discretion. This time span of descretion is based on responsibility, and the greater the time-span, the higher the evaluation of the job.

Jacques claims the following advantages for the time-span method. It is consistent, systematic and a means of analysing responsibility in jobs and executive organizations.[4] With payment in some sort of congruence with time-span of discretion Jacques believes that employees will consider remuneration to be equitable or 'felt-fair'.

Unfortunately, time-span has so far proved difficult to measure in practice, and many other factors worthy of remuneration are ignored. If employees reject discretion as a factor the whole scheme is rejected. The main weakness, however, must be the nebulous nature of the time-span concept.

Decision-banding

Decision-banding is an approach developed by Professor T Paterson.[5] The factor used is decision-making, and the ranking of jobs is based on the following six levels or bands of this factor:

1 Policy making
2 Programming
3 Interpretive
4 Routine
5 Automatic
6 Defined

These bands are divided into two grades (with the exception of Defined), the higher grades containing jobs which involve the co-ordination of lower grade jobs. Thus all jobs are supposed to be capable of assessment by comparison with the decision bands and grades.

The use of one factor ensures simplicity, availability for all jobs, and speedy implementation. As with time-span, however, other factors are ignored and the scheme is consequently somewhat inflexible.

Time-span and decision-banding have not proved to be popular job evaluation schemes and their application has been minimal. The factor can prove to be contentious, and certainly trade unions do not find the schemes wholly acceptable. In the last analysis, it is difficult to see how far removed these schemes are from the simple ranking or grading method, and they seem to offer no improvement on the inflexibility of these schemes.

Analytical grading

Analytical grading is associated with Doulton and Hay and has been used for managerial, technical and manual grades in the British Broadcasting Corporation.[6] It represents an attempt to combine the best features of multiple and single factor schemes. The five factors judgement, original thought, man-management, specialist knowledge and experience are used for white-collar jobs. Decisions, social skills and manual dexterity are added for manual jobs. Each factor is normally broken down into five degrees. The factors are not weighted, however, because the scores are not totalled. The rank order of the job is determined by that factor which has the highest score of the five or eight.

The basic assumption behind this scheme is that the company recognizes and remunerates high levels of competence only. In addition, if one factor is highly rewarded, it is assumed that the presence of other factors in the job is of a high order.

Advantages include its speed in application, and relative simplicity. Unfortunately, it may be subject to considerable dispute and grade drift. This arises from the problem that some jobs may enjoy a high ranking because of a high score for one factor, while others have the same ranking because of high scores in all five or eight factors. Such a state of affairs hardly leads to feelings of equity, and appeals for regrading are frequent.

A summary note on single factor schemes

At best we must conclude that the single factor schemes are interesting. Their application to date has been very limited, and the response of trade unions has not been positive. But such schemes remain necessary developments in the process of improving job evaluation.

Towards a final choice

In 1968, the National Board for Prices and Incomes (NBPI) reported that 23 per cent of a sample working population of six million were covered by job evaluation schemes. Of this figure some 42 per cent were in a grading scheme and 11 per cent in a ranking scheme. Thus rather more than half of employees in the survey were covered by a non-analytical

94

scheme. 43 per cent were covered by points rating and four per cent by factor comparison, and therefore, rather less than half the employees surveyed were in an analytical type of scheme. On the basis of organizations surveyed, rather than employees, the NBPI found that 47 per cent were using a points rating method, 28 per cent job classification, 20 per cent job ranking and five per cent a factor comparison scheme. On this basis the tables are turned with 52 per cent of the organizations surveyed using analytical schemes. The Board also found that analytical schemes were increasing in popularity, but did not report on the use of the modern methods.[7]

Some eight years later in 1976 the Institute of Personnel Management surveyed some 168 organizations to assess the frequency of use for different methods including the modern category.[8] The results of this work are presented below.

Table 1
Analysis of job evaluation schemes by employee groups

| Scheme | Use of the scheme by employee group (%) | | | | |
	Mana-gerial	Clerical	Adminis-trative	Skilled manual	Semi- and unskilled manual
Non-analytical					
Ranking	29	16	17	10	11
Grading or classification	26	45	30	19	21
Paired comparisons	9	12	9	6	7
Non-analytical Total	64	73	56	35	39
Analytical					
Points rating	39	63	54	40	50
Modern					
Guide chart profile	38	20	30	4	3
Direct consensus	4	4	5	2	4
Profile method	5	5	7	5	7
Modern Total	47	29	42	11	21

Source: Gill D. *Job Evaluation in Practice*, IPM, 1976

The relative popularity of the non-analytical ranking and grading schemes is obvious. But points rating, an analytical scheme, is overwhelmingly the most popular single method in use for all employee groups.

Organizations should choose one job evaluation scheme to cover all the jobs to be reviewed. This will reduce costs and complexity but more importantly ensures consistency and comparability across the organization and therefore goes some way to ensure a degree of equity in the minds of the job-holders. There are problems to be overcome in the use of one single scheme, however, because most job evaluation methods do experience difficulty in coping with simple (for example unskilled manual) *and* complex (for example managerial and professional) jobs. The traditional response to this situation has been the use of non-analytical ranking for the less demanding jobs and points rating for the more complex categories.

The problem of choice is further compounded by the admission that there is no evidence to prove that any one scheme is more accurate in terms of the results produced. Despite the expense of analytical and modern job evaluation schemes, the remuneration structures may be no more precise in reflecting job worth than an inexpensive non-analytical scheme. If one of the modern schemes is used, the client can be saved from the dilemma of choice because the consultants will probably offer their own scheme. But this may be inappropriate to the problems and conditions of the organization, particularly under the headings of technology, industrial relations and ability to pay. Additionally, the categories and range of jobs should influence the choice of job evaluation scheme.

Against this problematic background it is difficult to ignore the popularity of the non-analytical schemes of ranking and classification and the analytical scheme of points rating. Furthermore, these schemes have been effectively applied across the whole range of jobs likely to be found in employing organizations, more so than any other type of scheme so far developed. The only other schemes available which have enjoyed an equal degree of success are direct consensus and profiling; but with a very limited number of reported applications.

Accepting the need for a single method for all categories of jobs coupled with the likelihood of different levels of complexity in jobs, the requirement is for a scheme which can realistically and convincingly evaluate the whole range of jobs in an organization, if required. With the direct consensus method, less demanding jobs can be evaluated first with the paired comparisons approach; complex jobs can be dealt with by the factor approach if time allows, after experience is gained with the simple version. Thus the one scheme can provide quick and acceptable results within a flexible approach. The direct consensus method deserves more applications than it has had to date, particularly given the high order of participation which characterizes the scheme.

Implementation

The need for procedure

The introduction of job evaluation represents a major intrusion into some vital aspects or organizational life. Remuneration structures may well be altered as a result of the exercise and the climate of industrial relations will both influence and be influenced by job evaluation. Communications between management and employees are of some significance if job evaluation is to work smoothly, and the two parties should possess a clear understanding of the objectives, and steps involved within a mutual agreement on the acceptability and application of the scheme. The evaluation of jobs should be systematic, based on careful analysis of content and capable of translation into a logical structure of remuneration. To produce logical pay structures systematically, without detracting from the quality of industrial relations, requires careful attention to procedures within the job evaluation approach from the first stage of identifying need right through to the implementation of a definitive structure.

Purpose and strategy

A problem with current remuneration structures will often be the reason for introducing job evaluation. The question arises as to whether any systematic redesign of the structures should be limited to the short-term objective of dealing with immediate difficulties or the long-term objective of designing a payment system which is supportive to the wider corporate requirements of the organization. Such requirements would involve an appreciation of corporate purpose and the strategies underpinning its achievement by those involved in managing remuneration. A strategic approach to the management of remuneration was discussed in chapter 1, and was described as involving a systematic approach to decision making for wages and salaries. While not wishing to identify job evaluation as an element of corporate policy, it is reasonable to suggest that it represents a possible systematic basis for a remuneration strategy. The analysis of jobs, the comparison of job worth, a review of labour market rates and the design of wage and salary grades represent the steps in a rational exercise which could reflect and contribute to corporate need, certainly more so than the *ad hoc* and irrational response to uncontrolled pressures which have characterized so much of the history of wage and salary determination.

A strategic role for job evaluation is more likely to result in careful planning, effective communications, the choice of an appropriate method and a systematic style in the various stages of the exercise. The end result should be a set of pay structures which reflect the role defined for remuneration in the life and work of the organization.

Communications and involvement

Employees need to be fully aware of the objectives and implications of job evaluation. This should be a matter of course, both in the interests of employee relations and to ensure their co-operation at several stages of the exercise. Informing and involving employees should be a 'keystone' of management's approach to evaluation, and there is a case for introducing full participation. Participation at every stage will ensure that employee awareness is maintained. At the least, employees should be involved in, and therefore aware of, the preparation of job descriptions and should be members of the evaluation committee. As far as the wider labour force is concerned, the CAC has recommended that employees should be informed on the number of points for factors, the levels for points, the points ranges in the grades, the minimum and maximum points on the salary grades, and the means of determining starting salaries in each grade.[9] Certainly, it will be important for management and trade unions to be able to explain the following to the labour force: what job evaluation is; why it is to be used; how it works; how grades are determined; how individuals can appeal if they dispute the grading; the appeals procedure; the means of maintaining the scheme over time; and the incorporation of new jobs into the grading structure.

The trade unions will probably influence communications and participation, although it is difficult to define what their attitudes will be in different circumstances. The TUC took the view that union involvement should be somewhere between non-involvement (to reserve the right to challenge the results) to being fully involved in every stage.[10] Clearly management should approach the unions at the earliest opportunity to explain why job evaluation is considered necessary, to discuss the method to be used and the degree and types of communication and involvement. Staff unions may be eager to become involved, while manual unions may be initially indifferent and quite willing to leave management to set the pace. Assuming full involvement, management and union will probably jointly agree the composition of the steering committee, methods of communication, the method of job evaluation and the detail procedures, the composition of the evaluation committee, the form of the appeals procedure and the means of

98

monitoring the scheme over time. Additionally, the unions may wish to draw a very clear line between job evaluation and collective bargaining, leaving the former to measure the importance of jobs and the latter to determine the levels of remuneration for those jobs.

Steering committees

Initial management and union discussions on the terms of reference and method of job evaluation may be expanded and formalized into a steering committee composed of representatives from both parties. In the main, such a committee has responsibility for determining the purpose of job evaluation, planning the programme, deciding on the method, selecting the key jobs, choosing factors, points and weightings, checking the work of the evaluation committee (and co-ordinating if more than one committee is used), defining grades and designing the appeals procedure. Some of this work can be carried out jointly with the evaluation committee.

A chairman for such a committee could be a senior executive, personnel manager or consultant (although either of the last two, will probably be involved in chairing the evaluation committee). The senior executive is probably the most appropriate choice since he can report progress to the Management Director and Board and advise on the implications for company remuneration policy.

Evaluation committees

These committees or panels have responsibility for actually carrying out the heart of the exercise; the evaluation of the jobs and the construction of a rank order for those jobs. If a small number of jobs, or a single department is involved, one committee will be sufficient. In the case of several departments or multiple locations several committees will be required. More than one committee places pressure on the steering committee to ensure congruence and co-ordination in the work of the panels. One panel only is preferable, in order to ensure consistency throughout the evaluation exercise, although members will change over time to provide sufficient knowledge of the whole range of jobs. If the job evaluation can be slowed down, it may be advisable to work with one committee at a time. Alternatively, the steering committee will need to ensure that the committees work within common terms of reference which are clearly defined and understood.

The relationship between the steering committee and the evaluation panel or panels is vital to the success of job evaluation. In particular, both bodies should jointly determine the factors and the key or benchmark jobs: these should not be imposed on the evaluation panel but determined in the light of the committee members' knowledge of jobs and their approach to evaluation. In short, the evaluation committee needs to be involved with the thinking and decision-making of the steering committee as soon as a decision is taken on the method of job evaluation to be used.

The size of evaluation committees tends to vary between six and 12 members. The actual number is not important and may be based on the requirement to provide adequate representation for interested parties (particularly trade unions). Some degree of competence in judging should be a basis for selection. It is normal, however, for panels to be made up of equal numbers of management and employee representatives, and members should preferably be established by mutual agreement between management and trade unions. In some cases, particularly direct consensus method exercises, this writer has worked with committees of management and union representatives with a ratio of 2:1 in favour of the latter. This composition always proved to be effective because the results tended to be seen as 'union property' and commitment to the gradings by shop floor representatives was often complete.

Committees require a chairman, and the personnel manager or resident consultant should fill this role, which is normally non-executive. If the chairman has an executive role he runs the risk of having to cast a deciding vote on the rating of certain jobs where a unanimous decision cannot be reached. It is useful for chairmen to avoid such situations by delaying difficult evaluations until the committee has increased its experience and the number of ratings to which it can make reference. Preferably, such a decision should be made by the committee on the basis of the advice from a non-executive chairman.

Members of the panel should have a sound knowledge of the jobs and departments to be covered by the evaluation, and this may involve changing members for each department or location. They should also be thoroughly aware of the evaluation method and the processes involved, and this requires some provision of training, particularly in the areas of analysing jobs and rating them. The personnel department or the consultants should furnish the training. Additionally, colleges and universities can provide such services. Lectures and films can also be provided by the steering committee.

Within the training process it is essential that committee members are exposed to, and develop, common conceptions of the factors and the standards to be applied. It is useful to provide case studies giving actual examples of the evaluation method in similar industries.

The dynamics of evaluation committees are always problematical.

Some members can be more articulate than others, or just plain awkward, and this can cause bias in the rating. The chairman has a real responsibility for dealing with such problems by minimizing any discussion and guiding the committee so as to avoid any potential distortions. To ensure effective judgments the committee, should first assess the bench-mark jobs which represent the whole range of jobs to be considered. All jobs should be presented in a sequence which avoids large gaps between job values, as the committee members will tend to bridge the gaps by assessing the jobs closer to each other than should be the case. Finally, there should be a pleasant and co-operative spirit among committee members, which can generate an openness and willingness to work towards agreement.

Job descriptions

The use of job titles in the simpler methods of job evaluation such as ranking can create difficulties for the evaluation committee, because such titles are often too generalized and out of date. Furthermore, the same title may be applied to jobs of differing content, or different titles applied to jobs of similar content. Job descriptions are the means of avoiding these problems and should provide the raters on the committee with as accurate and clear a picture of the job as is possible. Nonetheless, the formulation of clear job titles can be a useful first step in the preparation of the job descriptions.

The work involved in the development of job descriptions can be termed 'job analysis' which embraces the following:

(i)   the collection of information on the content
(ii)   requirements and responsibilities within jobs
(iii) a statement of this information in the form of a job description
(iv)   the analysis of content, requirements and responsibilities in terms of the factors used in assessment.

Information can be collected by interview, questionnaires and observation. A combination of all three is desirable, but normally interviews and questionnaires are used if only to save time.

Job descriptions should contain the job title; the job title of the supervisor to whom the job holder is responsible; the job titles reporting to the job holder; the appropriate department or section or location. All tasks which the job holder is required to perform should be recorded together with a statement of purpose for each task. Some priority should be determined on the basis of importance, frequency, or sequence. Each task should be presented in a separate paragraph starting '. . . to prepare . . .' or '. . . to ensure . . .' or '. . . to supervise . . .' and so on, as appropriate. In the main, each paragraph should state what is done and why it is done. Where possible, tasks should be quantified in terms of frequency and time, or perhaps in physical terms such as financial values in connection with materials used.

A sample blank job description is provided in figure 6 on page 103 which clearly identifies the elements involved. It should be noted that the signatures for 'Agreed and approved by' should include management and employee representatives to record their agreement and should also record acceptability to the job-holder.

The analysis of job content is on the basis of the factors chosen for the scheme, and the job descriptions should be written in such a way that they provide the raters with a 'window' on the degree to which each factor is present in the job. Succinctness in the narrative of job descriptions, and careful choice of words, are essential if the evaluation committee is to gain the necessary insight to the job.

Accurate and well-written job descriptions are the foundation of effective results from job evaluation. But such descriptions represent an art and not a science. Subjectivity can never be completely eradicated. The interpretation placed on the job by the evaluation committee cannot be completely objective. Getting the facts right in a job description presents an opportunity for increased objectivity; but it cannot guarantee this.

In the case of managerial jobs there is a need to allow for flexibility in the job descriptions. Initiative, problem-solving ability and the necessary freedom to act in the interests of the company rather than the requirements of a job specification require a less structured approach to preparing the descriptions than is suggested above.

This may result in managerial job descriptions which describe a whole range of actions and responsibilities and which are presented in a straightforward and descriptive manner rather than slotted under different factor headings. The evaluation task will be much more difficult for the committee who must now 'read into the job' the degree of presence of the factors. To improve the rating effectiveness 'key areas' can also be defined alongside the job description. These identify the most important parts of the job and may be anything from three to eight in number depending on the level of management. Provided the key areas are adequately defined and described they may assist the evaluation committee in assessing the relative worth of managerial jobs more effectively than standard forms of job description. A possible job description and key areas for a works manager are presented in figure 7 on page 104 together with performance standards to explain the key areas.

Figure 6
Job description

Job Title: ....

Supervisor job title: Department:
Job titles reporting: Section:
                                          Date:

1   Tasks/duties:

2.   Plant and equipment used:

3   Materials used:

4   Extent supervised:

5   Training and experience required:

6   Working conditions:

It is agreed that this job description is a fair and representative
description of the job and sufficient to define its job content for the
purpose of job evaluation.

Prepared by: Date: Agreed and approved by:
                                                     Job holder:
                                       Union representative:
                                                     Supervisor:
                                          Personnel manager:
                                                           Date:

Inevitably the evaluation of managerial jobs will be provided with fewer yardsticks compared to other job categories. The job descriptions should never become a 'restraint' on management decision making and actions. Given these concerns the evaluation of middle and senior management jobs should be approached with caution.

Figure 7
Job description and key results

Job Title   *Works Manager*

Job Description
Responsible for implementing policy in the form of a production programme designed on the basis of production department capabilities, and information, controls and support from Product Engineering, Industrial Engineering, Works Drawing Office. The programme is determined to satisfy sales forecast and budgetary requirements with the co-operation of the Manager of Production Services to secure joint agreement on Services inputs to the process of achieving programme.

Considers output and financial targets in the process of preparing the production programme and identifies and provides for the adjustments of production resources and facilities (other than materials) in line with the programme. Materials availability is secured with the co-operation of the Manager of Production Services.

Determines policies and guidelines for recruitment and safety within Production, Product Engineering, Industrial Engineering, Works Drawing Office. Monitors procedures and communications for Industrial Relations.

Determines the policy for product engineering to provide for new products and modifications to existing products which are aligned with production capabilities. This policy should accommodate the Sales and Research and Development requirements within production parameters through effective liaison and co-operation with these functions. Policy for the Works Drawing Office and Industrial Engineering is designed to provide the appropriate data and information inputs which can support a flexible production programme for schemes while containing costs. Maintains co-operation with Maintenance to monitor the appropriateness of maintenance work to the production programme.

104

Statement of key area Costs	Performance standard
Productivity and output	When budget targets are achieved When output targets are achieved to schedule within pre-determined production capacity limitations.
Industrial relations	When disputes are minimized to a frequency acceptable to the Manufacturing Director.
Product Engineering	When new products and modifications to existing products are consistent with production capabilities.
Industrial Engineering and Works Drawing Office	When the co-ordination of costs, time, methods, product files and work measurement information provide a means of measuring and controlling production department performance, determining the work load and establishing a programme for non standard products.

Conclusions

The main argument in favour of using job evaluation is that if properly used, it provides a fairer basis for determining remuneration than *ad hoc* management decisions. There is also the issue of confidence in a systematic approach to pay determination and in the results. Management and employees often feel that the results of an evaluation exercise are fair, particularly with the more sophisticated schemes and the high order of analysis involved. Perceived equity can therefore be enhanced by the use of job evaluation. But 'felt-fair' results do not mean accurate results. They may represent more accurate structures than those going before, but job evaluation outcomes are inevitably the result of opinion.

This does not so much detract from the advantages of job evaluation but warns management and unions of the care with which evaluation must be handled and the degree of realism which should characterize their expectations of the results. These results are a rank order based on an assessment of job worth. The design of the remuneration structures to align with such ranking must now be considered.

References

1 NATIONAL ELECTRICAL MANUFACTURING ASSOCIATION, *Job rating manual and hourly job rating plan*. 1953.

2 TRADES UNION CONGRESS, *Job evaluation and merit rating*. Fourth edn. 1974.

3 JACQUES E, *Time span handbook*. Heinemann. 1964.

4 JACQUES E, *Equitable payment*. John Wiley and Sons. 1961.

5 PATERSON T, *Job evaluation*. Vols 1 and 2. Business Books. 1972.

6 DOULTON J *and* HAY D, *Managerial and professional staff grading*. Allen and Unwin. 1969.

7 NATIONAL BOARD FOR PRICES AND INCOMES Report No 83, *Job evaluation*. HMSO 1968.

8 GILL D, *Job evaluation in practice*. Institute of Personnel Management. Information report No 21. 1976.

9 ACAS Advisory Booklet No 1, *Job evaluation*. 1977.

10 TUC, *Job Evaluation and Merit Rating*. 1974.

Further reading

THOMASON G F, *Job evaluation: objectives and methods*. Institute of Personnel Management 1981.

UNGERSON B. *How to write a job description*. Institute of Personnel Management 1983.

5
Designing the remuneration structure

With or without job evaluation to determine rank order, jobs within an organization have to be priced. This involves the determination of pay grades and wages and salaries to be applied to such grades. Both external and internal considerations will influence this exercise, which requires a careful and logical approach if the remuneration structures are to reflect company policy. The elements to be embraced by the management of remuneration in designing structures are discussed in this chapter. Although reference is made to the role and outcome of job evaluation in the process of determining structures, discussions often treat the major features of design for consideration as an administered approach in their own right.

External considerations

Labour market surveys, of various kinds, are a means to develop information which provides organizations with an opportunity to construct competitive wage and salary structures. Such surveys can be categorized as follows:

(i)   Generally published surveys usually on a national basis such as those issued by Computer Economics Ltd and Lloyd Income Research

(ii) Remuneration survey clubs where several companies, usually up to 20, join together in the free exchange of wage and salary information. Sometimes the companies club together to carry out a labour market survey on an annual basis. Such associations are very useful, not just in terms of keeping in touch with market conditions, but in providing information to deal with immediate and particular problems. It is surprising that more companies do not initiate the formation of these clubs whether on a local, or regional or national basis

(iii) Commercial surveys are provided by many management consultancy companies. Hay-MSL actually use such a survey to formulate the grading structure developed in their guide-chart profile method of job evaluation which was discussed in chapter 5. PA offers a data bank based approach which uses computer processing to provide some match between the clients' jobs and those in the updated data bank. The validity of this data is enhanced by checking the remuneration levels against certain variables through computer based regression analysis

(iv) Published surveys, particularly by occupation, are more readily available than the foregoing. Reward Regional Surveys Limited are one source of such information and the publications of Incomes Data Services and Industrial Relations Review and Report provide useful records of pay settlements and developments. Another source, the *New Earnings Survey* is conveniently summarized in the Department of Employment *Gazette*. Managerial earnings are published annually by the British Institute of Management in the BIM/REL *National Management Salary Survey*. Many professional organizations and public sector bodies now publish earnings data for managerial, professional, technical and clerical staffs. A good example is the Institute of Administrative Management's *Clerical Salaries Analysis*

(v) International comparisons are more difficult to obtain, but some consultancy companies have developed information on remuneration levels in other countries. Additionally, the embassies of the countries concerned are sometimes willing to furnish information, particularly if it is available from government departments.

Whatever information is obtained on market rates of pay, management should use their judgment to determine its accuracy and usefulness as a basis for determining internal rates. It is here that a company remuneration policy can help in the process of determining the organization's 'market rate' or 'market stance'.

The results of surveys can be presented in varying ways, but bar charts for pay scales and ranges are common and readily interpreted. In addition to actual pay levels and ranges, the surveys provide analysis of the information in the form of median, upper and lower quartile levels for each job. An example of this form of presentation is provided in table 2 on page 109.

In the simplified bar chart in figure 8 (on page 109), the salary ranges can be identified at once and it is sometimes useful to superimpose on each company's pay range bar the quartiles and the median levels of pay.

Alternatively, a simple graph showing the trend for quartiles and medians is sufficient. Finally, tables, graphs and charts should be supported by the raw data on which they are based, to allow the client an opportunity to see how they have been formulated.

Table 2
Example of remuneration survey data presentation

Job: Works manager	Pay range in £s	Pay levels in £s
Lower quartile	£9,500–£10,800	£10,200
Median	£10,400–£11,850	£11,350
Upper quartile	£11,500–£12,850	£12,100

Assuming that a company has the necessary survey data for each job being assessed, management must define a salary range for these jobs by Graphical presentation sometimes provides far greater visual impact and an example is provided in figure 8.

Figure 8
Example of remuneration survey data presentation in graphical form

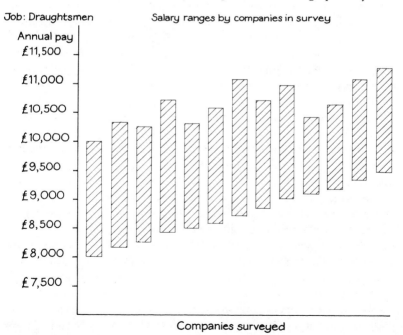

deciding midpoints first, and then upper and lower limits. These points will reflect the labour market position which management wish the company to adopt, based on their assessment of survey medians and quartiles. But this decision will require further qualification in the light of internal considerations.

How many structures?

A remuneration structure comprises the scales (and levels) of pay for different jobs. A few jobs, such as senior management posts, will have their own rate of pay, but the majority of jobs will be grouped into pay grades. In determining grades, management must be careful to design the structure to reflect and cope with organization characteristics, the influence of change, and the influence of labour market and collective bargaining pressures. It should also provide for motivation through opportunities for advancement and provide for perceived equity by ensuring consistent recognition and reward for job requirements across the grades.

The question arises as to whether one structure or several will be appropriate. Although one structure will provide the advantages of commonality, consistency and effective control, it is rarely appropriate except in small companies. Responsibility, in particular, is one characteristic which varies considerably, and thus senior executive grades should be separate from middle and junior grades. Technical jobs may require special skills, clerical jobs may have little in common with manual jobs, and so on. Organizations may not wish to adopt as many structures as there are occupations, but groupings for several structures will probably prove necessary.

Jobs which prove difficult to fill because of the nature of competition in the labour market will also require special consideration. Professional staff have proved a particular problem area in this context because their labour market tends to be nationwide and therefore offers a wider range of employment opportunities. One way of dealing with these occupational groupings is to evaluate jobs in terms of age, education and experience which are deemed to represent the number of years that have elapsed since the employee obtained his qualification. These years are a measure of 'maturity', and this technique is called maturity curve analysis. Salary survey data is used to determine the remuneration appropriate to levels of maturity within the company. Although this approach short-cuts the difficult process of determining professional salaries, it has proved contentious. It is essentially subjective, open to bias in evaluating the incumbent rather than the job and ignores comparability and equity with other jobs in the company. Furthermore, the technique relies on considerable accurate external survey data, which may not always be available in updated form.

We can conclude that several remuneration structures will normally be necessary to reflect the particular characteristics of different occupational groupings. At a minimum these will probably include the following:

(i)   management and professional
(ii) technical
(iii) administrative and clerical
(iv) supervisors
(v)   manual: skilled
(vi) manual: other.

Grades

Within each structure a number of pay grades will be required (excepting jobs with separate pay rates) and the number of grades will depend on the two following considerations:

(i)   Too few grades limit opportunities for promotion
(ii) Too many grades create complexity, duplication, prove difficult to control and are so close to one another as to prompt questions among employees about the fairness of pay differentials.

The number of grades which can avoid these difficulties lies between three and 10 depending on the circumstances of the organization. The more complex the jobs the greater is the number of grades with managerial grades often numbering 10 and manual grades numbering three. Grades should allow for the recognition of differences between jobs; should be equitable in the minds of employees; should allow for career progression and effective managerial control; and should help minimize disputes about pay.

Grades therefore correspond to ranges of pay, and their design and content in terms of remuneration ranges should reflect company requirements in the following areas:

(i)   differentials between ranges
(ii) overlap between the ranges
(iii) the number of ranges
(iv) the width of the ranges.

Differentials are the amounts of difference in money terms between the pay ranges. The greater the number of pay ranges, the more they will be squeezed together and the smaller the differentials. With fewer ranges, differentials are greater.

Overlap occurs between grades because there are too many grades within the total span of money, and because the width of the ranges is too great.

The number of ranges is determined by the lower and upper pay levels for the jobs in the structure. The size of the differentials required will also influence the number of ranges.

The width of ranges is the difference or span between the lower pay level and the upper pay level. It is normal to measure width or span in one of two ways:

(i)   as a percentage of the lower limit, eg a range of £3,000 is 50 per cent of a lower limit of £6,000
(ii) the difference between the upper and lower limits calculated as a percentage of the mid-point, eg a lower limit of £5,000 and upper limit of £8,000 results in a span of 46 per cent of the mid-point. The mid-point is £6,500 and the upper lower limits are £1,500 above and below this figure.

Determining differentials

We have already seen that the number of grades within a structure should be no less than three and no more than 10. Additionally, if the grades are to motivate employees through the provision of opportunities for promotion and the rewarding of different levels of factors within jobs, the differentials will need careful consideration and should ideally determine the number of grades. Differentials should be worth 15 to 25 per cent. Thus, if the lowest range of grade (A) in the structure has lower, mid and upper points of £5,000, £5,500, and £6,000 per annum respectively, then at a 20 per cent differential the next higher range (B) should have lower, mid and upper points of £6,000, £6,600 and £7,200 respectively. Note also that in this example there is no overlap between B and A. B's lower limit equates to A's upper limit.

Determining overlap

If we reduce the size of the differential in our simple exercise to 15 per cent we find an increase in overlap between range A and range B as follows:

112

	Lower limit	Mid-point	Upper limit	Overlap
Range A	£5,000	£5,500	£6,000	–
Range B	£5,750	£6,325	£6,900	£250 or 22 %

The amount of overlap at 22 per cent of the value of range B £250 ÷ £1,150 × 100) is indicative of the effect of reducing the size of the differential. To increase the differential to 25 per cent would actually push range B away from range A in value. Differentials and overlap are a matter of remuneration policy which will be returned to shortly.

Determining range
The width or span of a pay range also influences overlap and therefore the size of the differential. If we increase the span of range A and maintain a 20 per cent differential we find the following effect:

	Lower limit	Mid-point	Upper limit	Overlap
Range A	£3,500	£5,500	£7,500	–
Range B	£4,200	£6,600	£9,000	£1,500 or 31%

At a 15 per cent differential the overlap becomes 50 per cent of the range B.

It is difficult to define the optimum salary width without knowing the number of jobs and the size of differentials. Additionally, information and reported experience on the subject is scarce. In the late 1970s the British Institute of Management found the following average widths for white-collar jobs:

Senior management	25 per cent above and below mid-point.
Middle management	20 per cent above and below mid-point.
Clerical jobs	10 per cent above and below mid-point.

These figures give salary spans of 50 per cent, 40 per cent and 20 per cent respectively. In this writer's experience, a 50 per cent width is excessive and 20 per cent too low. Thirty to 40 per cent is preferable and workable giving 15 to 20 per cent above and below the mid-point. Anything above 40 per cent will normally be included to reflect merit and performance. Routine jobs rarely require widths greater than 30 per cent.

Balancing differential overlap and range
We have concluded above that differentials should be 15 to 25 per cent, and should produce a differential value between grades which avoids arguments about jobs which are borderline and also provides motivating increases in pay. If a constant differential is employed

throughout a remuneration structure, employees in the more senior positions may feel that differences in remuneration levels do not reflect increased responsibility and skill. This can be remedied by increasing the differential to reflect increasing demands in jobs. Thus at manual and clerical levels 15 per cent would hold, at middle management level 20 per cent could be the differential and at professional and senior management level, 25 per cent could be the figure. A finer scale for increases could be used if necessary.

Some degree of overlap in the pay ranges for grades is useful, for example to cover trainees in a grade. While in training, these people are worth less to the company than those doing a full and effective job at the top end of the lower grade. Such overlap is often a function of range width as we saw in the previous section. Overlap should preferably not exceed 50 per cent of the higher grade, and should only occur between two grades and no more. In excess of 50 per cent creates demotivation in the minds of those at the lower end of the higher range, and overlap between more than two grades results in misunderstanding and possibly dispute about gradings. To repeat, overlap should be used to reflect training and induction in the first instance and range spans should be designed to cater for this type of overlap.

The grades and job evaluation

The remuneration structure or structures contain the grades, which in turn contain jobs positioned on the basis of their worth to the company. That worth is determined by a review of the position of those jobs in the external labour market by means of some type of survey, and some assessment of their internal value which can usefully be carried out by job evaluation. Within the grade is a pay range with lower and higher limits, and the jobs within the grade have pay levels corresponding to the limits and are therefore of similar worth. The type of structure containing the grades will be designed to reflect the organization's requirements and policies. The issues involved can include the number of grades, differentials to cover reward and promotion, the width of salary ranges, and the degree of overlap between grades.

The design of a pay structure must inevitably be an exercise in judgment and compromise, in order to balance the pursuit of aligning the structure with remuneration policy in a rational and equitable form. Job evaluation, as a systematic process introduced in support of policy, provides a basis for designing the pay structure. In giving an example to this process of designing remuneration structures, the job evaluation method of points rating is used.

Plotting the scores

The end result of the work of the evaluation committee is a rank order of jobs based on points scores. The next step is to prepare a scattergram on which points scores are plotted against existing wages and salaries. With this scattergram, a line of best fit or trend line can be drawn through the points with an equal number of points (or jobs) above and below the line. Figure 9 below presents an example of such a diagram with trend line.

Figure 9
Scattergram with plotted job evaluation scores and trend line

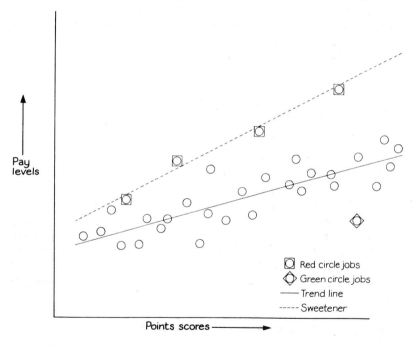

In theory, jobs above the trend line are overpaid and those below underpaid. Again in theory, the cost of bringing jobs up to the trend line should be balanced out by the savings derived from bringing overpaid jobs down. This of course will never happen in practice, but the trend line does reveal isolated jobs which are grossly overpaid and grossly underpaid, and management are thus able to decide what to do with them. There are three possible responses: the 'sweetener effect', the 'red circle effect' and the 'green circle effect':

The 'sweetener effect' refers to the raising of the trend line to absorb the higher paid jobs.

The 'red circle effect' refers to the freezing of 'overpaid' jobs until the trend line catches up and/or the evaluated worth of other jobs catches up through the normal process of movement through cost of living increases.

The 'green circle effect' refers to jobs which are well below the trend line but which cannot be raised to the line's level with justification. Usually such jobs have become superceded by developments in the firm, or the job holder is well below par in terms of competence and performance. Pay for these jobs is frozen until the incumbent retires or moves to another post. At this point, the job can be scrapped or filled by someone capable of a higher order of performance at which time the rate for the job may be raised to the trend line.

In practice the red and green circle effects tend to be adopted in the United States much more than is the case in the United Kingdom. Sorting out such anomalies may prove to be a lengthy process and can result in serious disputes. The 'sweetener effect' is obviously more practical. By implementing the results of job evaluation at the time of a general wage and salary increase (as indicated by the broken line in figure 9), it may be possible to arrive at a rational and balanced remuneration structure without increasing the remuneration of people who are overpaid in the terms of the job evaluation outcomes.

Determining the preferred remuneration levels

The trend line established by internal evaluation is compared with the rates revealed by the market survey, by plotting market rates on the same scattergram. As mentioned earlier, the market information plotted will depend on the position or stance which the company chooses to adopt in the market. It is assumed here that the company is interested in a position somewhere in the upper half of the range for market rates. Thus the medians and upper quartiles are plotted with the trend line, *see* figure 10 on page 117.

Management are now in a position to decide what they wish to do with the organization's trend line. With the market data known and plotted, the trend line can remain stationary. Alternatively, it can be 'sweetened' to varying degrees in order to move the levels of pay towards some degree of comparability to the actual levels of pay for similar jobs in the labour market. By using the 'sweetener' effect, a new trend line or actual remuneration line is established which can represent

116

Figure 10
Graph for comparing trend lines and market rates

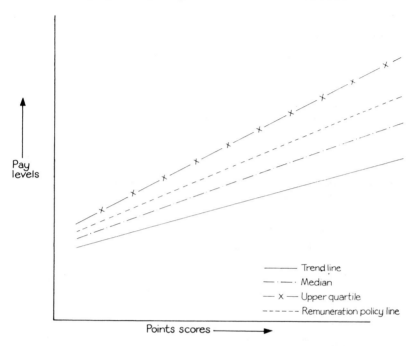

the market position preferred by management in the light of their internal remuneration policy considerations. This remuneration policy line is plotted on the graph (*see* figure 10 again), and the degree of slope represents the amount of promotion and career progression the company wishes to provide in the remuneration structure. It is now possible to translate the new remuneration line into a grading structure based on decisions about the number of jobs and grades, midpoints in the grades, the ranges, differentials, overlap and promotion policy.

Points into grades

With job evaluation, the points scores provide a basis for determining the grades which will embrace groups of similar jobs. This is not a straightforward exercise, however, and some trial and error may be necessary before the grading structure is workable. Management will need to test that the number of grades can accommodate the desired differentials without unwanted overlap and with acceptable range widths. All this will have to be accommodated within the new trend, or remuneration policy, line. The sequence of this experimentation begins by determining that the desired number of grades will hold with the desired differentials. Then the mid-points for each grade can be plotted on the new trend line on the basis of points scores. The breaks between the grades are determined on the basis of the range of points scores for each grade. Should there be a large number of jobs at the break points, the grades may require some 'rejigging' as breaks should occur where there are few jobs in the hierarchy of scores. If the break points remain among job clusters, it may prove necessary to alter the number of grades or the size of the differential. This issue of break points is important, because problems will arise in trying to slot all the jobs in the cluster into one of two grades which will result in appeals against the assessment by job holders who feel they should be in the higher grade. Again, grades should not overlap to avoid the problem described in the last sentence. Overlap is provided by the pay ranges which will be applied to the grades. Grades may be of equal span or range or may increase towards the upper end of the grading structure.

Grades into pay structures

Grades have now been determined on the basis of the points scores for jobs resulting from the job evaluation exercise. Finally, the pay ranges are determined for each grade to reflect the earlier decisions on differentials, range span and overlap.

Thus two exercises have now come together to provide a remuneration structure:

(i)   the grading of jobs on the basis of their worth to the company by means of job evaluation
(ii) the determination of pay levels for those grades in the light of external comparisons coupled with the internal policy for remuneration operationalized in terms of pay levels, ranges and differentials.

Figure 11 on page 119 presents this approach in graphical form, by showing the determination on the grades on the trend line by points scores. Table 3 on page 119 presents the differential, span, and overlap in the pay ranges. Figure 12 on page 120 presents the final form of graded remuneration structure.

Wages, salaries and employee performance

One addition to the procedure described above for the determination of grades is some allowance for recognition of employee performance. For salaried staff, the trend line which is used to determine grades will correspond to the annual (or weekly, or fortnightly or monthly if

118

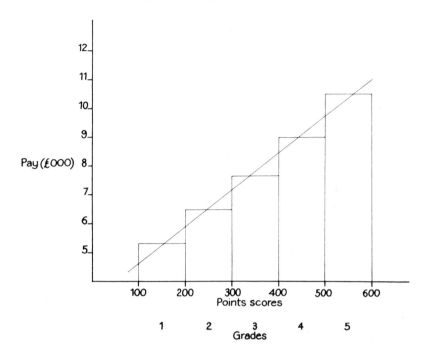

Figure 11
Determining grades by points on the trend line

Table 3
Defining and applying pay ranges to the
points graded structure

Points range	Grade	Differ-ential	% Span	Mini-mum £	Mid-point £	Maxi-mum £	% Overlap
100–199	1	–	30	4,760	5,600	6,440	–
200–299	2	15%	30	5,474	6,440	7,406	50
300–399	3	15%	30	6,295	7,406	8,517	50
400–499	4	20%	30	7,554	8,887	10,220	36
500–599	5	20%	30	9,065	10,664	12,264	36

The above example is very simple and assumes one grading structure only, but the translation of points scores into pay grades through the use of differentials, spans and mid-points for ranges is clearly shown with the accompanying degree of overlap. The conversion of this data into the pay grades determined on the new trend line is shown below.

119

Figure 12
The graded remuneration structure

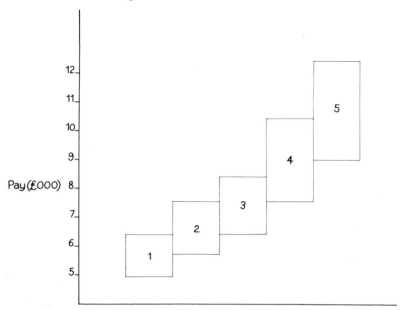

From the above chart is is possible to see how the grades increase in width towards the upper end of the scale.

deemed appropriate) gross salary figures net of any additions including overtime, where paid, and merit. Merit schemes are discussed in some detail in chapter 8, but it is important at this stage to mention 'merit caps' as shown by the broken lines in figure 13 on page 121.

These merit caps represent the additional range of pay which may be paid on the basis of performance appraisals. As with the basic range of pay, the merit range increases in span towards the upper end of the scale.

In the case of wages for manual grades, the trend line and therefore the grades and their pay ranges, also correspond to basic pay net of premium payments. What is important here is the absence of any bonus payment, and it is difficult to add ranges for piecework payments to the grade ranges as with 'merit caps' for salary ranges. The consolidation of premium payments is a development which allows for manual grades to be structured in the same manner as salaries.

A systematic approach to the determination of wages must include grading for basic rates, coupled with some system for dealing with bonus payments. This brings in issues of production control, work

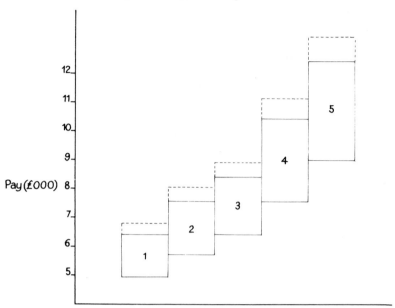

Figure 13
The use of merit caps in the grade structure

measurement and incentive payment design; matters which are deferred to the next chapter. The fact that basic blue-collar remuneration is capable of effective structuring opens up the possibility of improved structuring of bonus payments in addition.

Maintaining remuneration structures

Any structure, whether or not determined by job evaluation, requires continual review if it is not to decay. A job evaluation exercise will require regular evaluation of new and changed jobs to determine rates of remuneration which allow for comparability with rates for existing jobs and demonstrate consistency in the use of job evaluation. It is also likely that rates of pay, and therefore the grading of certain jobs, will be challenged by the incumbents. Employees who consider that the demands of their jobs have increased will press for regrading.

These pressures require an adequate response, which can only be provided by anticipation of problems: a process requiring continual review. This in turn requires an appeals procedure which allows for an assessment of jobs individually. It should also provide employees with the recognized right to appeal through a management and union agreed appeals procedure, and involves the establishment of an appeals committee (usually of six members) to determine whether appeals should be processed. In the event that the committee feels the appeal is justified, the job is re-evaluated and accordingly regraded.

It is normal for the appeals committee to handle new or changed jobs in order to carry out assessments and allocate the jobs to the appropriate grades. In these cases new or altered job descriptions will be necessary. The actual evaluation can be usefully achieved by comparing the new jobs with the benchmark jobs assessed in the original evaluation exercise.

The appeals committee may have to meet regularly; perhaps once per month immediately following the introduction of the new grading structure, settling down to once every three or even six months. In addition, a review of the remuneration structure should take place every year to assess the regradings, the effects of the introduction of new jobs and changed jobs. The review should also determine that the movement of jobs is consistent across the grades and that the grades are holding and are still relevant.

Every three years the wage and salary structures, and the job evaluation if used, should be audited. Such an audit should check on any drift in the grades, such drift occurring in the form of expanding pay ranges within the grades, which results in narrowed differentials and increased overlap. The job evaluation method should be examined to check whether the benchmark jobs and the factors and weightings are still valid or require updating to reflect new job demands brought about by technological developments or organization change.

Grade drift is the most common problem with analytical and modern methods of job evaluation. Indeed, regrading and the resultant drift can be a problem for systematically determined pay structures, whether or not determined by job evaluation. Thus structure redesign and the 'revamping' or replacement of the job evaluation scheme may become necessary every five years. Any scheme will lose 'bite' over time, and there is a limit to the modifications which can be incorporated. At least with a rational approach to the design of remuneration structures, the organization will more readily identify the need for change and introduce that change.

Conclusions

This chapter has outlined the elements of a systematic approach to the design of remuneration structures which has also embraced the contributions of job evaluation. Job evaluation is useful because it offers method, strategy and helps to concentrate the mind on procedure and results. Where managements experience difficulty in organizing their responses to requests from employees for a more rational grading structure, methods of job evaluation prove useful. Management are not relieved of the responsibility to monitor, and if necessary check any deterioration in the resultant structures over time. It is not the case, however, that the systematic determination of pay structures always requires the job evaluation methodology. The elements of design such as external surveys, determining differentials, range widths and the final grades are not dependent upon job evaluation as a pre-requisite. But we can question management's ability and opportunity to construct viable structures which meet the expectations of employees, and more importantly, are accepted as fair by those employees without job evaluation. Job evaluation seems to build a bridge between management and workforce which allows them to agree on the acceptance of new remuneration structures as well as the means of determining them. But the structures so far defined are for basic pay only. Attention must now turn to the issue of reward for performance and its implications for the design of remuneration structures.

Part III

INCENTIVES

6
Incentive schemes: principles and objectives

Incentive payment schemes represent an attempt to influence the behaviour, and therefore work performance of employees, through the provision of a monetary or non-monetary reward which is extra to basic remuneration. This reward is assumed to bring forward a level of contribution to the company which is greater than that normally forthcoming in return for basic pay. Such payments, or bonuses, can be made for extra effort on the shop-floor, shouldering extra responsibility in the office, selling more than quota in the sales division, and achieving increased profits in the boardroom. In one form or another therefore, incentive schemes can be applied to all categories of work, although the majority of the effort to develop and improve incentive schemes has tended to concentrate on methods suitable for shop floor production based schemes. Incentive schemes have proved popular in the United Kingdom, more so than in any other industrial nation, and in some industries represent a considerable proportion of the task of managing remuneration. Although up-to-date figures are not available, research and surveys in the late sixties suggested that more than three quarters of firms in Britain used incentives and more than one third of the nation's labour force was covered by some form of scheme. This figure has not fallen in the intervening period; indeed interest in incentive schemes grew during the late seventies. For the individual on incentive, the payment can represent a significant element of earnings. For the trade union, incentives are a subject for negotiation. For management, the incentive scheme is deemed to offer some hope of a reduction in unit costs of production. Very seldom, however, is this translated into some measure of improvement in corporate performance. It is a paradox that reward for employee performance has not been linked to the strategic approach to company well-being. A review of origins, principles and objectives of incentive schemes follows as a basis for understanding why and how these schemes are packaged and used.

Origins

It is difficult to determine exactly when and where the first industrial type of incentive was designed and offered. The dissolution of the craft guild system in the sixteenth century (by an Act of King Edward vi) saw the rise of a system of merchant capitalism in which workers were hired to work at home for an income based on piecework. Such a system survived to the end of the eighteenth century when the industrial revolution brought the age of the factory. The factory system did not see the introduction of incentives until the end of the nineteenth century, and such schemes are associated with the Scientific Management Theories in general and F W Taylor in particular, who introduced the 'merit differential piece rate' for cyclical or repetitive work in 1884. By the beginning of the twentieth century the names of Halsey, Emerson, Gantt and Bedaux could be attached to a list of schemes aimed at improving worker performance, improvements which were rewarded by some form of financial bonus. It is from such origins that today's work measurement based incentive schemes have grown.

The age of the factory and urbanization saw the rise of the department store with hired sales staff. Apparently not documented, the idea of commission on sales must have surfaced during the latter half of the nineteenth century, with employees paid a flat rate or percentage of the value of the goods sold. To this day commission survives as a financial incentive for sales personnel at all levels, from shop assistant to sales executive.

The nineteenth century also saw the introduction of the non-monetary incentive. Several industrialists, such as Robert Owen and Seebohm Rowntree, saw the importance of worker welfare as a contribution to employee motivation and performance. Rowntree can be credited with introducing a pension scheme, participative procedures for drawing up and monitoring work rules, and the employee representative role. All of these proved means of improving worker contributions to the performance of a confectionery company which certainly prospered.

Incentive schemes, therefore, have a long history, and financial incentives for the shop floor have been subjected to considerable development in the course of the past 80 years. The appearance of schemes between 1875 to 1925 was significant. The rise of Scientific Management Methodology in this period, aimed at the organization and administration of industry, provided the tools for building incentive schemes. Such schemes and their underpinnings served much of British industry well for many decades, although they have perhaps been clung to for too long in some industries with damaging results. In this connection, incentive schemes can be broken down into traditional and modern types. Because the schemes attempt to provide a reward or payment for results it is normal to use the term Payment by Results (PBR) to generally describe them.

Principles

The incentive has traditionally been an addition to pay provided for additional effort or performance. Basic pay is remuneration for the time the employee spends at his employer's disposal. Thus, incentives are offered to improve the level of worker performance to levels which management consider necessary to maintain a required level of production. Worker performance may be defined in the quantitative terms of effort (measured in terms of time or physical output), some target to be achieved or a broader grouping of elements including skill, responsibility and general behaviour. The first type of measure is normally used in schemes for blue-collar employees (such as piece-work), the second type in management schemes (such as profit sharing and sales bonuses), and the latter in white-collar schemes (such as merit rating). The incentive scheme should cause management to ask what they want of their employees in terms of a performance based contribution, and to determine how much they are prepared to pay for it.

Incentive schemes are an intervention in the process of behaviour at work. They are based on the assumption that employees are indifferent to corporate needs and require some 'carrot' to bring forward positive and contributing behaviour. It is not often considered necessary to create conditions which will help and allow the employee to change attitudes. Instead, the negative attitudes tend to be 'smothered' by the reward in the hope that they will cease to be an obstacle in the relationship between worker and corporate need. In these terms, incentive schemes are concerned with the structural elements of the working environment and aim to modify employee behaviour. Designing in 'behavioural' elements to more positively influence behaviour has proved difficult in practice. The objectives of technical excellence in work measurement, such as production control and scheduling and pay design, have long needed to be balanced by 'behavioural excellence', in the form of a financially and socio-psychologically motivating environment where high levels of performance are permanently maintained. Lacking such an environment, the

129

majority of schemes have tended to provide only a temporary improvement in employee performance.

The reward may be provided to the individual in recognition of his personal effort or results. Such a direct and individual approach has long been preferred in shop-floor and management schemes. Alternatively the reward may be distributed among a group of employees on a pre-determined basis. This approach has been used with shop-floor schemes, but has been more popular with white-collar schemes. In recent years, there has been some interest in the provision of group rewards with the addition of an extra payment to reflect individual performance. At the present time, this method is growing in popularity.

Reward must be based on performance, and therefore measures of employee contribution are required. These measures have normally been found among the techniques of work measurement for shop-floor operations, and in the form of measures possessing less precision for white-collar work. Profits and sales values have been used for executive schemes. Value added has more recently been used as a measure for blue-collar and white-collar schemes.

The payment of the reward should be close in time to the achieved performance. For manual schemes the payment has usually been in the same weekly pay packet, and for white-collar employees in the next salary payment. Some recent schemes, particularly of the value added type, have not met such a requirement and the results have been decidedly mixed.

Objectives

The objectives for incentive schemes should be clearly defined, understood and agreed by management and employee representatives. Additionally, such objectives should be worth while and should represent significant gains in company performance for management, and in motivating after-tax rewards for employees. The reward should therefore be a real incentive, bringing forward demanding levels of effort and performance and providing for earnings which exceed basic pay for the time rate by a substantial margin. Determining the size of that margin requires some effective judgement on management's part if the incentive effect is to be achieved. Traditionally shop floor schemes were designed to provide a bonus of some $33\frac{1}{3}$ per cent of basic pay at the least and certainly anything less than 25 per cent of basic pay is not going to influence performance to such a level that the costs of the incentive scheme are absorbed. This is a particular problem with white-collar methods such as merit schemes, which often add little more than three or five per cent of basic pay. Although employee performance may improve with such schemes, it may be due to reasons very different from any incentive effect deriving from the reward.

It is an obvious requirement that incentive schemes of any type should be self-financing yet this is often ignored in practice. The costs of work measurement and preparatory work, coupled with the cost of any bonuses, can be considerable and savings within production and arising from the better utilization of staff should balance, if not exceed, these costs.

Set standards of performance should be achievable by employees of average ability. This will require test runs by the work study department to prove to shop-floor employees and shop stewards that this is the case. Additionally, normal conditions in jobs covered by any incentive scheme should provide the employees full opportunity to work effectively, and thus maximize incentive earnings. Machine down-time or general interruptions to work should be mimimized and should not affect the size of the bonus. In providing for these conditions to be met, the preparatory work should identify and remove or allow for any problems likely to influence earnings potential. The amount of reward should only be determined and agreed with the unions when the levels of performance appropriate to the incentives have been measured in the light of all possible conditions which can influence employee performance.

Incentive schemes should be readily understood by managements, unions and employees, and therefore simplicity in the method is preferable to complexity. Employees should clearly appreciate how bonus is calculated and therefore what is being paid for and by how much.

The financial reward or bonus is designed to improve employee effectiveness at work, and this should be matched by improved utilization of equipment, services and more effective production methodologies and organization. Thus the schemes should not concentrate solely on the quantitative aspects of the work place. Qualitative elements require attention, and this extends in particular to the management of production in connection with incentive schemes for manual groups. The quality of production information and decisions should be improved on the basis of financial and physical production data needed for the scheme. This improvement in the data base for production management should also contribute to improved effectiveness at the level of supervisory management.

Schemes can be usefully introduced through the normal processes of collective bargaining, preferably within a participative framework to ensure shop-floor commitment to the performance and pay standards. The levels of bonus will need to be determined with reference to national and local agreements as well as the plant level agreements. At the least, the incentive payment will probably be a percentage of the basic pay determined in such agreements.

Considerations for white-collar schemes

The majority of schemes for white-collar employees provide a bonus to employees linked to performance as is the case with shop-floor PBR. The issue of achievable levels of performance is therefore as important to white-collar schemes as to manual schemes. The criteria used to quantify performance may be in terms of achieved results, or in terms of an appraisal of the demonstrated capabilities of the individual. Care is needed to ensure that in the latter case assessment is as objective as possible. Findings should preferably be supported by a more precise measure of performance in terms of work load, cost savings or if possible work output. It is inescapable, however, that the means of determining white-collar performance is problematic except in cases where sales and profits can be used. Clerical work measurement schemes have been developed to deal with the problem, but they remain limited in terms of application.

Length of service has been one popular determinant of white-collar incentives used in salary progression schemes but it is doubtful if this provides any real incentive effect in terms of raising performance. The main consideration in such schemes appears to be the provision of an inducement to the worker not to change his job, rather than some stimulus to greater contribution. Indeed, the majority of white-collar schemes provide a much weaker incentive than the more popular shop-floor methods. They may require a greater degree of management control of performance than has been traditionally the case with manual schemes, although managerial intervention has often proved necessary even with the most generous shop-floor rewards.

Longer term issues

The relationship between payment and performance often proves difficult to maintain over time. Regular reviews of pay and performance standards should take place, preferably every 12 months. If the relationship is distorted it may be necessary to redesign or even replace the incentive scheme. A consensus of opinion in firms known to this writer suggests that schemes need changing every three to five years in order to reawaken the incentive effect.

Indirect incentives and benefits

Some incentive schemes offer a weaker incentive effect than financial reward. Indeed such schemes as profit sharing and employee shareholding are indirect incentives in that they are designed to improve the employee's commitment to the organization, while recognizing a higher order of need than immediate cash. Such a recognition can create a positive climate for employee attitudes to the company, which in turn facilitates the application of direct monetary incentives and their influence on employee work performance.

The provision of long service awards, suggestion awards, expenses, subscriptions to private health schemes and company cars also represent indirect incentives, although they are also classified as employee benefits. The incentive effect of such benefits is not as clear or as strong as direct monetary rewards, and their influence on behaviour is usually soon lost when they have been awarded. As an immediate and short lived incentive they need careful timing in their application. Other non-monetary incentives can include working conditions, canteen and recreation facilities, education and training. The problem with this kind of provision is that widespread application has diluted any incentive element which may anyway have been minimal in the first place.

Experience in the United Kingdom points overwhelmingly to a preference for cash rewards amongst the workforce. Indirect incentives have not been as popular, and excepting profit sharing and employee shareholding, are more properly described by the term 'employee benefits'.

Payment and performance

There are three basic questions to be asked by management and trade unions in their approach to the subject of direct financial incentives:

(i) what level of payment should employees earn?
(ii) how hard should they work for that payment?
(iii) how hard can they work?

As we have seen in earlier chapters the answer to the first question depends on a mix of issues including labour supply, the relative bargaining power of unions and management, the economic health of the industry and the expectations of the labour force. The second question is equally difficult to answer. Management may be clear about how hard they want their labour force to work, but the employees determine a pace of work which may be acceptable to them but at variance with management's aims.

Faced with difficulties in the control and determination of pay levels and the effort exerted by labour, management have found some confidence by adopting work measurement as an answer to the third question. This confidence has derived from the view that measurement reveals how hard people can work and these findings have been extended to determine the level of reward for such effort. Thus within an incentive scheme management are paying for measured effort on the basis of three assumptions:

(i) measured effort equates to the maximum level of effort forthcoming from labour
(ii) employees are willing to contribute to the achievement of corporate objectives through a financial inducement
(iii) effort varies in relation to earnings.

All three assumptions are open to question. The maximum level of effort is tied up with the issue of how hard should people work and, as mentioned above, this is not under the control of management. In the case of the second and third assumptions, we must remember that money is not the only motivating factor and social factors should also be taken into account.

The effort bargain

Thus financial incentive schemes represent no more than a bargain. They result from a compromise of management and employee beliefs about effort (manual) general ability or performance (white-collar) and pay. Incentive payments reflect conceptions of pay and effort and measurement, in whatever form, must seek those performance and pay levels which allow for compromise to be achieved. The question of whose objectives are met by incentive schemes cannot be easily answered. Both parties are looking for gain, and more than in any other facet of employment, it is here that management urgently need to ensure that the labour force achieves its own objectives of higher levels of earnings and standard of living, while simultaneously contributing to the achievement of corporate objectives. Therefore the incentive scheme needs careful management in the interests of corporate well-being, and the assumption that the incentive alone can ensure results is untenable. The acceptance of this has been lacking in many incentive scheme applications, with inflationary results.

An incentive scheme specifies a level of reward and a level of effort. Management's task is to ensure the permanent balance of the two. Given that they are determined by compromise rather than precision, this must give rise to doubts about how such balance can be achieved, and the overwhelming evidence proves that at best it has proved difficult. Against the background of this knowledge, there are many people inside and outside British industry who believe that incentive schemes should be put aside and replaced by consolidated time rates. Such a move would replace a compromise based on the understood but complex exercise of designing an incentive with a compromise based mainly on little understood pressures influencing general earnings levels.

Employee performance and corporate well-being

The potential of incentive schemes has always been considerable, but too many organizations have limited the advantages to the short-term expedient of satisfying employee demands for more money, performance issues being pushed into the background. Companies have preferred to pay lip-service to the translation of the provision of reward into corporate performance. Yet an incentive scheme can have dramatic effect on the financial state of the enterprise, and not just because of the immediate effects of an increase in productivity. The following figures are taken from an actual incentive scheme and give evidence to the potential scope for corporate financial gain.

Example to show full financial gains
deriving from a production incentive scheme:
monthly pay-roll.

Improvement in productivity deriving from the scheme at 20% by moving direct employee performance from an effort rating of 69 to 83 on the British Standard Scale (14/69 × 100)

Fixed and variable overheads at £90,000 or 72.5% of the monthly payroll.

Fixed overheads at £40,000 or 44.5% of fixed and variable.

The increase in output was valued at £10,000 per 4 week period. The reduction in unit labour costs was £16,000 per 4 week period. In addition the over recovery on overheads was £8,000 per 4 week period calculated as follows:

£124,000 × 72.5% × 44.5% × 20% = £8,000

Over a 48 week period the savings from the scheme were £408,000 or 20 per cent of an annual revenue of £2 million. In too many cases, management have difficulty in calculating unit cost savings and the over recovery. But armed with such information they may feel more

135

obliged to manage incentive schemes in the interests of long term company well-being, rather than the solving of a particular shop-floor industrial relations problem.

Useful terms

The shop-floor of industry has witnessed continual developments in incentive schemes for the best part of this century. It is here that the greatest sophistication in the design of schemes has been attempted, and the greatest complexity has resulted. To simplify matters it is useful to note that there are four variables at the heart of these schemes which require some measurement:

    (i)   measured work
    (ii) unmeasured work
    (iii) operator (employee) performance
    (iv) departmental performance.

Getting to grips with these four issues goes some considerable way to the situation where management can achieve the following:

    (i)   confidence that they are obtaining the operator and/or departmental performance they are paying for
    (ii) a measure of production system performance which can have relevance to the overall corporate requirements.

In brief, incentive schemes should provide information as a basis for improved decisions about production and performance. Of course, elements of working life which are divorced from the incentive payment will also influence employee behaviour and performance. But, with the appropriate and effective production information developed for the incentive scheme, management should be in a position to deal with those other issues on the basis of what objectives, in terms of productivity, they need to achieve if the incentive scheme is to be successful.

    Therefore, the following short glossary of terms used in connection with production incentive schemes is offered, as an explanation of such terms, and as a kind of checklist for the measures (and resultant information) which should be developed by management.

Measured work: Work for which performance standards have been determined by work measurement techniques.

Unmeasured work: Work for which no performance standards have been determined.

Attendance time: The total time spent by an operative at the place or places of employment, whether working or available for work, for which payment is made.

Measured time: That part of attendance time during which an operative is engaged on measured work.

Unmeasured time: That part of attendance time during which an operative is engaged on unmeasured work.

Non-productive time: That part of attendance time during which an operative is not engaged on productive work.

Standard hours produced: A time-based measure of the amount of work produced, expressed in terms of standard hours.

Unmeasured credits: A measure of the amount of standard hours credited for the amount of unmeasured work produced.

Non-productive credits: A measure of the standard hours credited for non-productive time (normally non-productive time caused by reasons outside the workers' control).

Total credits: A measure of the total standard hours credited for payment purposes (normally calculated daily or weekly).

Operator Performance index: An indication of the effectiveness of an operator whilst employed on measured time only.

$$\text{Formula for calculation} = \frac{\text{Standard hours produced}}{\text{Measured time}} \times \frac{100}{1}$$

Department performance index: An indication of the effectiveness of an operator whilst attending the place or places of work.

$$\text{Formula:} \frac{\text{Std. Hrs. Produced} + \text{Unmeasured credits}}{\text{Attendance time}} \times \frac{100}{1}$$

Pay performance index: An indication of the effectiveness of an operator for payment purposes only.

Formula:

$$\frac{\underset{\text{Produced}}{\text{Std. Hrs.}} + \underset{\text{Credits}}{\text{Unmeasured}} + \underset{\text{Credits}}{\text{Non Productive}}}{\text{Attendance Time}} \times \frac{100}{1}$$

Department average operator performance index: An indication of the effectiveness of all direct operators in a department.

Formula: $\dfrac{\text{Total Std. Hrs. Produced}}{\text{Total Measured Time}} \times \dfrac{100}{1}$

Trend performance index: An indication of the moving average level of any PI calculated over a period of four weeks.

Formula:

$$(\text{Last trend PI} \times .75) + (\text{Current PI} \times .25)$$

Conclusions

Incentive schemes may be worthwhile, and relevant to a performance orientated remuneration policy if they are effectively managed alongside other influences on employee performance. Much of British industry is characterized by an incentive 'culture', (whether rightly or wrongly is another matter) and on balance there is no hope of removing that culture at present. If incentives were to be put aside, no one could guarantee that current levels of performance would be maintained across the labour force let alone increased. Furthermore, much control data for productivity and costs would be lost. Incentive schemes are, therefore, very important and worthy of consideration in depth. The following chapter discusses the major schemes which are available. Chapter 9 provides an evaluation of those schemes and synthesizes the characteristics of the effective incentive system.

7
Incentive schemes: current practice

There is a bewildering array of incentive schemes to cover all groups of employees. In the following assessment, schemes are grouped into the following categories: traditional payment by results, modern payment by results, schemes for white-collar and managerial staffs, and new developments. The basic features of the various schemes are presented, although in the interests of conciseness it is sometimes necessary to describe general features of a particular group of schemes. It is inescapable that some understanding of the fundamentals of work study (better termed industrial engineering) is a prerequisite to PBR schemes on the shop-floor, particularly time study, rating and pre-determined motion time systems such as Methods Time Measurement.

Traditional payment by results (PBR)

Schemes under this heading are normally time-based and piecework derivatives. (Piece-time bonus systems, which are based on the principle of management and employee sharing any financial gain from any improved production, are mainly popular in the United States and enjoyed minimum application in the United Kingdom). They are based on job fragmentation, repetition, piece rate pay and individual worker reward for effort. Clearly they rely for success on the assumption that a financial reward can cause an increase in worker effort, and consequently, an increase in the level of productivity of the enterprise. Thus the worker must be able to vary his output in some kind of relationship to the effort he exerts. Accepting that this kind of relationship exists, management and unions have approached PBR as a means of determining both the level of effort which management should expect from the labour force and the reward which the labour force should expect from management. Underlying this is the assumption that worker effort varies in proportion to the level of earnings. Some precision is brought into the process of defining the effort-reward relationship, and it is here that the techniques of work measurement have perhaps played their greatest role in British industry, and made their greatest contribution. Although this is not, perhaps, the place to discuss the matter, it can be argued with some conviction that this has been a very limited and short-sighted use of work measurement.

Direct production work has been measured to provide the rates of effort which can normally be expected with a time rate (the effort forthcoming in return for basic pay) and the standard of effort forthcoming with the provision of a financial incentive. The history and development of work measurement has provided means of measuring effort and defines *Normal* rates without incentive and *Standard* with an incentive. This approach has been adhered to in PBR schemes for most of this century and to a considerable degree still influences the design of more modern incentive schemes. The technique for measuring effort is rating based on scales. Two such scales are in use in Britain. By far the most popular is the British standard scale (*see* figure 14 below) where normal effort (without incentive) is deemed to exist at 75 and standard effort (with incentive) at 100. For illustration we can note that the 75 equates to a walking speed of 3 miles per hour and standard, or 100, equates to 4 miles per hour. The second system in use is the Bedoux scale with normal at 60 and standard at 80.

Figure 14
British standard scale of rating

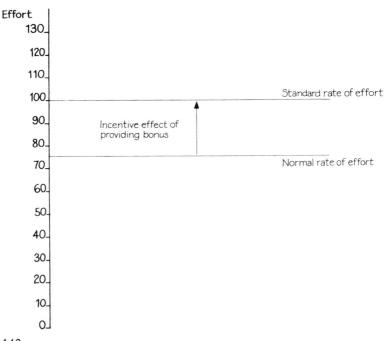

In theory, bonus is designed to raise effort by $\frac{1}{3}$ from 75 to 100 on the rating scale. The theory is that this $\frac{1}{3}$ improvement will be forthcoming for a bonus which represents $\frac{1}{3}$ of basic pay. The industrial engineer is trained to use rating as a means of determining just how hard people are working, although to what kind of tolerance is often difficult to determine. A five to 10 per cent tolerance may be expected depending on the type of work being studied.

Procedure

The rating is used to determine the level of effort before the incentive is introduced. A rate of 100 is not automatically introduced, however, as no one works continuously at 100 and not everyone can work at 100. Therefore observed rates are coupled with observed times taken to complete the task and are adjusted to a standard rating through the process of 'extension'.

This calculation is as follows:

$$\text{BASIC STANDARD TIME} = \frac{\text{OBSERVED TIME} \times \text{OBSERVED RATING}}{\text{STANDARD RATE}}$$

For example, if a task has an observed time of 12 seconds at an observed rating of 70 on the British standard scale, then the basic standard time should be as follows:

$$\frac{\text{OBSERVED TIME 12 SECS.} \times \text{OBSERVED RATING 70}}{\text{STANDARD RATING 100}}$$

$$\text{BASIC STANDARD TIME IS 8.4 SECONDS.}$$

A REST ALLOWANCE AT 15% GIVES STANDARD TIME OF *9.66 seconds*

It is not thought reasonable to expect a worker to maintain basic standard rate through the working day and a relaxation allowance is normally built into the basic time at 10 to 15 per cent. Therefore, in our example the time for the job would have to fall from 12 seconds to 9.66 seconds for the worker to be paid incentive.

It should be noted that work measurement measures the time taken to complete tasks in fractions of a minute called centi-minutes. Short tasks or elements of procedure are found in highly repetitive work, and take up to eight centi-minutes (0.08 minutes) with anything below 5 centi-minutes creating considerable difficulties for measurement. Medium tasks or element procedures are found in semi-repetitive work and take from eight to 50 centi-minutes (0.08 to 0.50 minutes). Long tasks or element procedures last longer than 50 centi-minutes (0.50

minutes+) and are found in highly skilled manual work such as polishing and detailed hand work such as painting pottery.

The incentive scheme may be based purely on time saved or may have times converted into units or pieces produced. The latter are popular and are normally called a standard time rate, or standard hour plan, or piece-time rate. In cases where time, and indeed work measurement are not involved in the determination of effort workers are paid a fixed sum for each unit produced irrespective of time taken to produce the unit. Such a scheme is called straight or fixed piece rate.

Time-based incentive schemes of the type discussed above have long been regarded as providing a *strong* incentive effect by linking remuneration to worker effort. The standard time-based schemes are the most desirable because the requirement for work measurement involves comprehensive analysis of the work situation and the provision of production control and standard cost data based on achieved standard times. Additionally, these schemes allow different rates to be set for different workers. This last point is a key feature of traditional PBR, ie the emphasis on the individual employee.

Traditional PBR, or rather the traditional work measurement techniques on which it has been based, has not proved successful in measuring the work in indirect tasks, such as storekeeping, maintenance, supervision and cleaning. The answer to this problem has normally been found in the form of a bonus which reflects the performance of direct workers. This bonus is normally paid as a percentage of the average paid to directs and is applied collectively. Because it is paid in lieu of a production bonus, the term 'lieu bonus' is occasionally used to describe this type of payment. Such schemes have not proved satisfactory, either to workers or management, although they are often applied in industry.

Developments

There are some seven or eight million workers whose earnings are influenced by traditional PBR. Schemes are introduced to overcome the 'nil incentive' effect of time or basic rates. Traditional PBR has developed away from time rate and piece rate schemes to provide an improved share of the benefits accruing from improved worker effort between management and worker. These 'developed' schemes have been designed to lower production costs, tighten up on measurement of work, and increase the opportunity for employees to improve earnings. Some of these schemes are briefly discussed below.

Halsey and Halsey-Weir methods provide for high rates of earnings but require effective and well controlled measurement of work (rate fixing). Proceeds are shared on an equal basis between management and employee.

The Rowan system was designed to cope with jobs which are difficult to measure.

The Atkinson and Allingham systems are suitable for trainees and low performance workers in an attempt to boost production. Once incentive effect is achieved, a more demanding scheme should replace this type.

The Bedoux system has proved popular in the repetitive and standardized work of mass production technologies, which have well developed production departments and ample control data. Such schemes are rarely given the name Bedoux, however. One industrial engineer told me that the name, when pronounced, sounded too much like a piece of continental plumbing!

Differential piece rate and accelerating premiums are complex in design and provide for an acceleration in the progressive rate of bonus as worker performance increases. Originally aimed at compensating for higher taxation on higher bonus earnings, these schemes are often used for the purpose of achieving high levels of output. The degree of sophistication required in the preparation of data is difficult to understand, and the schemes have not proved popular in Britain.

The sharing of benefits between worker and management as offered by several developed schemes has not been attractive to trade unions. In many traditional engineering firms piecework has held sway because of its promise of higher earnings and the considerable incentive effect. It is impossible to estimate the proportion of piece rate, time rate and developed schemes in British industry, but it is safe to say that piece rate or piecework is the most popular and widely used of the traditional PBR schemes. The developed schemes have arrived because of problems with traditional PBR; these problems are as follows:

(i) The subjectivity of rating and its openness to dispute
(ii) The emphasis on individual performance and payment.

Rating
Rating is not a precise enough measure of worker performance to provide a 'watertight' basis for the calculation of bonus. It is also an

essentially inconsistent technique in that varying rates of effort can occur between raters and between locations and jobs. The result of these deficiencies is often doubt about the fairness of the schemes in the minds of employees which can lead to dispute with management. Therefore, any claim for a precise causal relationship between the levels of pay, effort and output is difficult to substantiate in practice. For example, rating cannot determine the level of human effort exerted in a task if output is mainly determined by machines. These weaknesses in rating are particularly acute with the popular straight line proportional pay system where payment is by each individual performance or rating point. Rating is not accurate enough to provide such a fine-scale reliable measure.

Individual employee bonuses
Individual employee bonuses to reflect the individual performance of each worker covered by PBR has often resulted in as many pay structures as there are employees in the company. Hand in hand with this complexity comes the problem of differentials in earnings which are so many in number that comparability problems and disputes have proved inevitable.

Difficulties in justifying measures of performance and in controlling remuneration policy and structures have proved too burdensome for many managements (and shop stewards), and the fifties and sixties saw a considerable increase in the documentation reporting the failure of traditional PBR. In an attempt to provide an alternative approach to incentives, rather than dropping them altogether, new schemes appeared based on changes in work practices and the introduction of group incentives.

Productivity agreements

At the time of growing dissatisfaction with traditional PBR a form of management and trade union agreement on pay and issues related to productivity appeared in the form of the Blue Book Agreement at the Esso Fawley Refinery on Southampton Water. Throughout the sixties interest in productivity agreements spread like wild fire, helped by special provisions for these agreements in the incomes policies of the 1965 to 1970 period.

In their most sophisticated form, productivity agreements entailed jointly determined improvements in methods of working and the organization of work, paving the way to technological change and improvements in productivity. Thus productivity agreements were an attempt to remove traditional obstacles to technological change by involving the unions in the process of change and giving them the opportunity to exercise some influence on the results of change, both pleasant and unpleasant. In return for a contribution to the process of facilitating change, the employees received a share of the benefits accruing from increased productivity in the form of an increase in pay. Quite often a package was negotiated which included an increase in pay plus improved benefits.

One important feature of productivity bargaining which needs emphasis is the change in the nature of collective bargaining represented by the more sophisticated agreements. Conventional agreements tend to determine pay increases on the basis of such factors as the cost of living, comparisons with other firms, past increases in productivity and the resolving of conflict between the interests of workers and managers. Productivity agreements (in ideal form) represented a process of shared problem-solving on the subject of manpower contributions to technology changes, which were paid for ahead of their actual achievement.

The benefits of these agreements were shared between management and workforce. In management's interests, the productivity improvements were supposed to exceed the increase in labour costs to the extent that the financial inducement for labour should be accompanied by lower production costs, greater volume and improved profits.

Main areas of change involving the labour force tended to be in the following areas:

Quantity of work eg speeding up machinery, elimination of tea-breaks easing of restrictions on output.

Nature of work eg increased flexibility between skills and jobs, job enrichment.

Re-arrangement of working hours eg reductions in overtime, and changes in shift patterns.

Manning eg Reduction of numbers employed, elimination of craftmens' mates.

Organization eg new supervision structures, reorganization of work groups.

Methods and plant eg the introduction of new plant and equipment, the reorganization of production processes and the introduction of new techniques of work measurement and of method study.

By 1969 and 1970 there was considerable evidence that comprehensive agreements had achieved some degree of change in the above areas. But the reduction of overtime was probably the most widespread development achieved by consolidation of overtime payments into time or basic rates.

This process of consolidating premium payments was one way in which productivity agreements could have contributed measurably to the rationalizing of remuneration structures across whole ranges of British industry. Unfortunately this opportunity had been completely lost by the end of the sixties. There is little doubt that the decision of the 1964 to 1970 Labour Government to allow pay settlements within productivity agreements to exceed the norms for pay increases in the various incomes policy white papers, resulted in a massive growth in the number of spurious productivity agreements. Managements and union representatives put together incentive schemes which were no more than traditional PBR 'dressed up' to convince overworked Department of Employment officials that the increases in pay were justified because they were part of a productivity agreement. The demise of the National Board for Prices and Incomes and the abandoning of incomes policy witnessed the end of productivity agreements.

Productivity bargaining was a most ephemeral technique for determining incentive payments linked to productivity. In examining the reasons for this short life, reference must be made to difficulties in satisfactorily measuring productivity, the lack of evidence that these agreements had any appreciable influence on the level of productivity of the firm or the nation. One is faced with the inevitable conclusion that the price of productivity bargaining in terms of increased earnings would not have been sufficiently contained by productivity improvements to avoid a contribution to wage drift and cost inflation. It is therefore, unfortunate that potentially worthwhile objectives for productivity agreements were lost in the rush to meet incomes policy requirements. It is depressing to reflect that in the vast majority of organizations, the management and unions were unable or unwilling to face up to the demanding task of improving the management of remuneration in the pursuit of corporate well-being.

Modern payment by results

More lasting alternatives to traditional PBR have been the types of day work scheme which also grew in popularity during the sixties. Unfortunately these schemes have not matched the longevity of piecework, and a move away from them was clearly discernible in the middle to late seventies. Nonetheless in their day, they were considered to be the ultimate alternative to traditional PBR and a sound basis for re-vitalizing wage systems, collective bargaining and industrial performance.

An important feature of day work schemes is the emphasis on group or plant-wide payments as opposed to the payments for individuals in traditional schemes. (At least one management consultancy organization has attempted day work schemes for individuals but reports on their effectiveness are not available.) Thus it was hoped that these newer schemes would provide for a greater degree of rationality in incentive payment structures, and would drastically reduce the opportunities for disputes on the issue of comparability. The motor industry, in particular, saw some considerable applications of day work schemes, as did the light and medium engineering sector of industry. British Leyland's scheme, at the Cowley Oxford plant, regularly featured in the media in the early seventies, although more often than not for the wrong reasons (including strikes about the incentive payments and their application).

There are three categories of day work schemes worthy of note, and they have normally been applied to manual work only:

Controlled or measured day work involves a fixed standard bonus for a fixed level of worker performance applied to groups of employees, or sections, or departments, or indeed the whole plant. It is possible for these arrangements to be applied to direct and indirect employees. This type of day work scheme has proved the most popular in terms of reported applications.

Graduated or stepped day work provides a whole range of pay and performance levels and is usually applied factory wide. The most developed form is the premium pay plan which requires the development of a pay and performance matrix with job grades determined by job evaluation and performance determined by work measurement. Workers are able to increase earnings by improving their performance as well as by moving up to jobs of greater degrees of complexity and responsibility. These schemes are able to provide a greater degree of flexibility in earnings and performance, and they have proved to be the most successful and durable of the day work systems.

147

High day or time rate schemes offer a consolidated and high level of pay linked to the employees commitment to work at a performance level determined unilaterally by management decision. In many respects, this follows the pattern employed in many North American companies, but it has not proved popular in Britain.

When introduced, all the day work schemes claimed to offer the opportunity to develop rationalized incentive payment structures, thus giving management more control over labour costs than was the case with traditional PBR. Employees have normally benefited in the short run from an across the board increase in earnings. In the long run they have benefited (one hopes) from stability of earnings brought about by the fixed incentive payment; from fewer interruptions to work flow through improved production planning and management; and from the knowledge that workers expending the same effort in similar work were receiving the same level of bonus.

Characteristics of day work schemes

Day work schemes are formally negotiated between management and unions in order to get away from the 'looseness' and pressures of shop-floor bargaining which determines rates of effort and pay in more traditional methods of PBR. Formal procedures and standards are mutually agreed by management and employee representatives to cover performance, earnings levels and the design of the disputes procedure. Joint agreement is also necessary for the method of determining the causes of poor worker performance and the remedial steps to be taken.

An improvement in the quality of supervision has often been claimed as an advantage of day work. The foreman is required to monitor the achieved performances of operators on a daily or weekly basis, and more importantly has the responsibility for ensuring the existence of the conditions necessary to allow workers to perform at the required standard. With management committed to paying a pre-determined bonus, the importance of securing agreed performance is paramount. Performance is, therefore, usually agreed between foreman and worker. This is unlike traditional PBR where the agreement is normally struck between the worker and a rate-fixer who has the responsibility to fix times for work but no authority to ensure the conditions necessary for the worker to achieve standard performance.

There are four main requirements in day work schemes which are essential for success:

(i) the employee should recognize and accept an obligation to perform based on the equity of his financial reward

148

(ii) information about performance levels should be accurate and up to date

(iii) an increase in the number of supervisors and a clear definition of their responsibility for worker performance.

(iv) with specific and pre-determined pay levels the control of labour costs is in management's hands who should quickly diagnose and rectify the causes of substandard performance.

Advantages

The advantages for management which have been claimed to accrue from day work can be summarized as follows:

(i) rationalized pay structure replaces the chaos of piecework differentials

(ii) opportunity for improved control of production costs (through the containment of labour costs)

(iii) improved opportunities for increasing manpower and plant utilization

(iv) opportunity to improve production data flow to meet management's information requirements

(v) improved production control

(vi) shop floor negotiation replaced by centralized higher level negotiations reducing pressure on supervision and shop stewards and opportunities for dispute

(vii) standardized earnings levels can lead to the calculation of standard costs

(viii) labour costs can be related to production schedules

(ix) reduction of the work load in the wages department and production control.

The above improve the management of production and the manpower and physical resources. It is management's task to translate this into improved productivity.

Advantages for the work-force claimed for day work are summarized below.

(i) mutual agreement on: standard performance
                                          work assignments
                                          manning levels
                                          flow speeds

(ii) an 'across the board pay increase' at implementation

(iii) stability in earnings and financial security

(iv) reduction of 'comparability' problems relating to pay

(v) reduction in interruptions to work flow through improved production planning
(vi) a pay structure that is felt to be equitable
(vii) reductions in working week and amount of shift working
(viii) earnings levels higher than those outside the pay system.

It must be emphasized here that many of these advantages have proved difficult to achieve in practice. This has usually been because some of the following conditions have been absent in organizations introducing day work schemes.

Conditions necessary for success
(i) effective production planning and control of work flow
(ii) stable market for goods and services
(iii) co-ordination of work levels between departments
(iv) commitment of senior management
(v) commitment of foremen
(vi) acceptance of need for flexibility by the work-force
(vii) consistent output from all workers
(viii) work mainly machine-based
(ix) closely linked operations
(x) high standard of quality control
(xi) primacy of planning and control of production accepted by all managements in the organization
(xii) cost effective work measurement system
(xiii) work measurement system readily understood by management and workforce.

In the 1960s, the National Board for Prices and Incomes saw day work schemes as the answer to the problems associated with traditional PBR, and in particular piecework. But in reality, these newer schemes have run into serious difficulties, mainly because management have been unable to secure the conditions required for success. These conditions have been unattainable because the fixed pay levels offer no opportunity to reward individual levels of performance and because day work is appropriate to mass production technologies and not the traditional engineering sector of industry where piecework schemes have continued to operate.

Of the problems leading to the decline in popularity of day work, fixed payments and the resultant lack of flexibility to reward different operator performance levels stand out as the most serious. Where companies have opted for a consolidated day rate, employees have soon begun to demand a return to individual incentives. In this connection, it is interesting to note that the premium pay plan offers the flexibility so often seen as essential but missing in other types of day work schemes coupled with a rational approach to structuring remuneration. Furthermore, this type of scheme has proved very successful in practice, and it is somewhat surprising to note that its application has been limited.

The premium pay plan

With jobs classified by means of job evaluation and times for the operator to complete tasks determined by work measurement, it is possible to determine pay levels on the basis of performance levels and job requirements. The main advantage deriving from this approach must be the consolidation and rational structuring of basic pay *and* the premium payment for performance, providing management with a high level of labour cost control and giving what amounts to an equitable 'career structure' for employees. Not all companies will be able to adopt such a structure, but the principles are well worthy of close consideration.

It is normal for performance to be measured on the Bedoux or 60/80 scale rather than the British standard scale. Within each range of job classification are found consolidated rates of pay established for the range of performance from 70 to 90 on the Bedoux scale, in 5 steps. Additionally, 3 steps of performance are provided for training. Training is continued until a performance of 70 is reached and maintained for a minimum of two weeks. Thereafter the employee can elect to raise his performance and earnings levels. It is important to emphasize that payments should be consolidated for all hours of attendance.

Table 4 below presents a simple matrix for a premium pay plan.

Table 4
Premium pay plan matrix of pay and performance

Pay level	Performance levels		Job classification				
	Bedoux	British std	A	B	C	D	E
1	Training	Training	40	56	70	80	100
2	Training	Training	42	58	75	90	110
3	Training	Training	44	60	80	100	120
4	70	80	50	65	85	110	130
5	75	90	55	70	90	115	135
6	80	100	60	75	100	120	140
7	85	110	65	80	105	125	145
8	90	120	70	85	110	130	150

NB The amounts of payment are in £s per week

Bedoux and equivalent British standard scale ratings are provided. The pay structure is based on ranges determined by the job evaluation exercise but each range contains remuneration levels determined by work measurement. Such a structure is capable of effective control and provides a continuous incentive coupled with the flexibility of paying directly for individual levels of employee performance.

As in all day work schemes, the work study department checks worker performance levels on a regular basis, and failure to meet the agreed performance target results in a fall in earnings only when it is established that the reasons are within the employees' control. Even then, down-grading to a lower pay/performance level (or lower job classification) is not actioned until the employee has been given a reasonable length of time to regain his targeted performance level.

The most famous application of the premium pay plan was in the Philips Electrical group of companies. 12,000 workers were originally covered by the scheme and an analysis of poor performance revealed the following:

Operator responsible (condoned) 2 per cent.
Operator responsible (actionable) 8 per cent.
Management responsible 25 per cent.

These figures reveal a great deal about the implications of adopting day work schemes, and indeed about any rational approach to the structuring of remuneration. The pressures placed on management to maintain the conditions necessary for the achievement of targeted performances and the containment of labour costs are considerable. Weak and inefficient management will therefore soon find itself in serious trouble with its adoption.

Schemes for managerial and white-collar staffs

Although day work schemes sometimes covered indirect employees as well as direct, it has been traditionally the case that the encouragement of white-collar commitment to the success of the organization has been founded on schemes peculiar to these employee groupings. Such schemes have included bonuses, salary progression, merit rating, profit sharing, shareholding and cash allowances.

Bonuses for management

Supervisory staff may be paid a weekly or monthly bonus on the basis of the output of the department, or the achievement of departmental standard hours. These arrangements are made possible with the use of traditional PBR schemes. With day work schemes, the foremen normally receive a payment which is equivalent to the incentive element paid to the people they supervise. This arrangement can extend to inspection and test personnel. Additionally, bonuses can be paid to foremen on the achievement of delivery targets, for reducing departmental costs, improving quality and reducing waste. In connection with this last point it might be useful to design a bonus scheme for test and inspection personnel where amount of bonus depends on the effective checking of 'shoddy' work.

Bonus schemes for senior executives are very popular and vary widely in nature and scope. The majority, however, are based on company profitability and are either distributed on a group basis or to the individual. In the latter case, individual profit or turnover targets provide the measure of success and can usefully be determined within a management by objectives scheme. It is becoming popular for such bonuses to be pensionable, and the reductions in marginal rates of income tax introduced in the spring 1979 budget have enhanced the attractiveness of bonuses as methods of increasing the real amount of disposable income. Some examples are described below.

Bonus fund schemes provide a bonus from profits, or cost savings, which exceed a pre-determined target. Bonuses are normally distributed as a proportion of salary on a group basis. Although normally limited to directors and senior managers, the schemes may be applied to middle management if deemed appropriate.

Bonus schemes for individual executives are normally based on the standard of performance achieved by the division, department or function for which the executive has responsibility. A performance target must be determined and some means of measuring performance, such as return on capital employed or value of output, is required to determine individual effectiveness. For further discussion of executive bonuses the reader is referred to the final sections of chapter 8.

Bonuses for sales staff are often overvalued by organizations and certainly evidence suggests that they are not the pre-requisite to sales performance as traditionally thought. They are of two types; commission based on sales volume and commission based on contribution to the costs and profits associated with the sales of products or product groups. Commission can be distributed on a group basis or related to individual results. Since commission is added to basic salary, it is important to ensure that this salary on its own is sufficient to provide for financial security.

Christmas bonuses have traditionally been popular in the finance and retailing sectors, and normally equate to one week's salary. The payment of a thirteenth month bonus at Christmas is practised in a few organizations, and is one month's salary in the form of a 'Christmas box'.

Bonuses in kind are the provision of goods, travel and luxury items in the attempt to provide a short term improvement in sales and senior executive performance. A veritable industry has now developed to meet company needs for such services, and its growth suggests that incentives in kind are extremely popular.

Schemes for clerical workers

The design of salary ranges to provide some form of progression in earnings has sometimes been used to provide the incentive effect of achieving the next higher grade job. Alternatively, group incentives have been used in offices, based on the measurement of work volume over a particular time period. Individual incentives have been based on work which can be measured such as typing, processing of documentation and punched-card operations.

Salary progression takes place within a salary range for the job, on the basis of experience or merit. Progression on the basis of experience is normally through fixed increments awarded at regular intervals in line with the individual's service. Such an approach is widely used in public sector organizations. For example, in the British university system, lecturers move through a salary range of 16 steps with each increment worth some 6.66 per cent of the minimum salary in the range. In the simple example in figure 15 on page 155 increments are worth 9 per cent of the minimum salary in the range.

One major advantage of fixed increments has been provided by government policy because the increments can be paid in times of a pay 'freeze'. This decision was based on the grounds that incremental systems are held to be self-financing. The assumption is that people are leaving the organization and therefore the salary range, with salaries which are greater than those joining the scale. Whether this happens in practice is doubtful. Nonetheless, unions prefer these systems, considering them to meet the requirements for equity and an annual pay

154

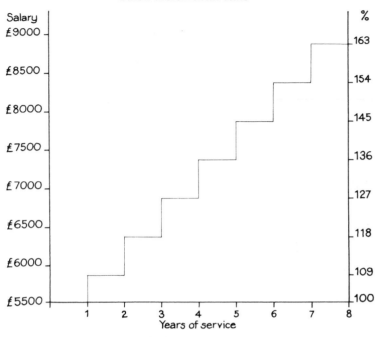

Figure 15
Fixed incremental scale

award, while management find them easy to control.

It is doubtful that fixed increments provide any incentive effect since the poor performer receives the same size pay increase as the 'high flyer'. Some flexibility has been introduced in the form of 'performance bars' which cannot be passed if employees are below par; by doubling the increments paid to the more effective staff; and by introducing a special 'add on' bonus for such people.

Merit and incentive

To provide the incentive effect missing in fixed increment schemes requires the adoption of a scheme which provides progression on the basis of employee merit. This involves the use of performance appraisal or merit rating which although done on an annual basis should desirably be carried out continuously. Although these methods are not necessarily part of the management of remuneration (they are often used for promotion purposes, deciding who needs training, and drawing up redundancy lists), and accepting that there are strong reasons for keeping money and appraisal separate, the salary review can usefully benefit from appraisal information. With performance related schemes

155

some definition of performance assessment is required, perhaps along the following lines:

excellent or outstanding or ready for promotion
very good or very effective or exceeds job requirements
satisfactory or adequate
barely satisfactory or struggling to meet job requirements
unsatisfactory or totally unsuited to the job.

Five grades are often used to provide the most effective spread for assessment purposes although there is always a danger that an indecisive or less brave manager will opt out and choose the middle grade. Therefore the use of four grades may be preferable where doubts exist about managerial competence in handling the assessments. Factors which are considered to be elements of the performance required by the organization must then be determined and these might include the following: judgement, knowledge, organizing ability, relationships with others, attitudes, initiative, supervisory ability and written expression. Points can be awarded as shown in table 5 below:

Table 5
Appraisal scheme with points score

Factors	Grades					Score	Final grade
	Excellent	Very good	Satisfactory	Fair	Unsatisfactory		
Judgement	25	20	15	10	5	15	
Knowledge	25	20	15	10	5	20	
Initiative	50	40	30	20	10	40	
Supervisory ability	25	20	15	10	5	20	
Written expression	25	20	15	10	5	25	
					TOTAL SCORE	120	Excellent

The factors may be apportioned equal points values or they may be weighted as in the case of 'initiative' above. Non-point systems may be used, in which the assessor provides a written assessment of the individual against the factors. Appraisal can also be carried out by the rank-order or forced distribution method, where each employee is ranked by class; these classes are normally defined in percentage terms as follows:

top 10 per cent
next 20 per cent
next 40 per cent
next 20 per cent
bottom 10 per cent.

No matter which method of assessment for white-collar staff performance is used, it is necessary to define percentage increases in salary for the total scores or assessments. These scores will fall into the performance categories of excellent, very effective, satisfactory, barely satisfactory and unsatisfactory. This will then provide for incentives to be paid in one of the two ways discussed below.

Merit rating schemes
Merit rating schemes provide an additional personal payment above the basic salary for the job. Against each of the performance categories an appropriate merit rate of pay will be established. Scores in each category may directly relate to percentages of pay, eg 0–25 points (unsatisfactory) no increase, 26–50 points (barely satisfactory) 2–5 per cent of basic pay, 51–75 points (satisfactory) 7.5 per cent, 76–100 points (very effective) 10 per cent and 100–125 points (excellent) 12.5 per cent. Or a straight points to money conversion may be used with 0–25 points receiving no bonus, 26–50 points receiving £2.50 per week, 51–75 points receiving £5.00 and so on. In both methods of determining bonus, the levels can be stepped to reflect the differentials in performance.

Performance related salary progression schemes
Performance related salary progression schemes do not provide a bonus as such, but take the performance category scores to determine the increments to be paid to the individual employee and therefore his rate of progression through the salary range for his job. To facilitate this the performance categories may be allocated an increase which is a percentage of the salary, as follows:

Assessment	% Salary Increase
Excellent	10.0
Very effective	7.5
Satisfactory	5.0
Barely satisfactory	2.5
Unsatisfactory	No increase in salary

Alternatively, the increase may be a percentage of the minimum salary of the range. It is usual to apply limits to salary progression which allow a maximum time limit to reach a maximum salary level within the range. Figure 16 below provides an example of such limits.

Figure 16
Salary progression with time and salary limits

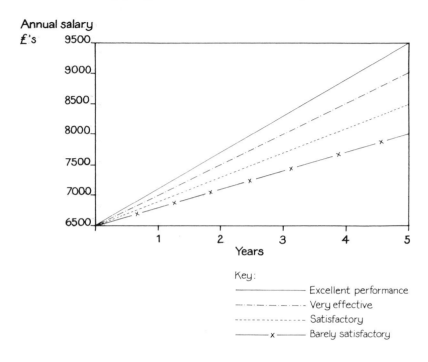

Salary progression and the need for planning

The successful introduction of salary progression depends on well designed salary structures, therefore a rational rather than an *ad hoc* approach to the determination of salaries and reward is required. Employees can be appropriately rewarded for their contribution to the performance of the organization, and enjoy the incentive effect of being able to expect progression through and between salary ranges. Furthermore, a foundation is provided for career planning, and therefore the future retention and development of effective employees, and the effective management of costs associated with salaries. As with so many incentive schemes, this process requires skilled management, not just of remuneration but of people's careers and the interpretation of the degree of success achieved in those careers now and the success likely to be achieved in the future.

158

Profit sharing

With this type of arrangement management and employees agree a payment, which is additional to wage and salary, dependent on the profits of the company. Such a payment may be in the form of cash or stock, and is usually made annually. The principle behind this approach is the need for recognition of the employee's contribution to the profitability (performance) of the company. The hope is that the employee will identify with the corporate objective of success and well-being in return for the goodwill demonstrated by the board in providing the share of profit and facilitated through a better understanding of the nature of the business and the requirements for success. Cash payments are normally determined through some value added formula, and the reader is referred to the section on value added later in this chapter.

The 1980 ammendments to the 1978 Finance Act may result in company stock becoming more popular, because the tax concessions now favour this method. Directors may not participate. Employees become eligible after one year's service. Payment in cash terms may be a fixed standard amount for all employees covered, or a percentage of basic pay or a percentage of earnings increasing with length of service. Executives are normally paid in proportion to their achieved performance as discussed earlier in the section on bonus schemes. The size of the cash award tends to be between two and 10 per cent, although in the case of executives can exceed 15 per cent of salary.

Profit sharing is not widespread and suffers several limitations, not least of which is the absence of the main requirement of incentive schemes: that payment be made close to achieved performance. Payment every six or 12 months hardly meets this requirement. Also ineffective workers share equally with the effective employees, the payments are often very small and lack significance in the mind of the employee. The payment may fluctuate from year to year, and thus may become an unreliable element of earnings.

Employee shareholding

Designed to motivate employees to identify with shareholders' interests, shareholding is increasing in application for senior executive groups in particular. Such methods are also called co-partnership schemes. As mentioned, in the section on profit sharing, the tax concessions provided in the 1978 Finance Act are relatively generous for this type of incentive provision and have helped widen the popularity of this approach. The British Institute of Management Survey Report No

41, *Employee Financial Participation*, provides more details of the provisions of the Act. Any firm considering employee shareholding will require expert advice on tax matters in the design of the scheme, which must be submitted to the Inland Revenue for approval. As with profit sharing, it is hoped that employees will identify with the interests of the business and gain a better understanding of company affairs.

Some debate has attached to whether employees really want shares, or prefer to sell them to obtain the cash. Employees' views on the security of the shareholding and the fluctuations in share values may be a problem. Taxation on dividends and the problems associated with shareholding employees who leave the company often reduce employee enthusiasm and create administrative tangles for management.

One form of employee shareholding which should be mentioned is the share option scheme in which over a period of years a block of shares is reserved for an employee to purchase at present market rate. If share values rise, the employee gains and tax concessions are allowed under the 1978 Finance Act.

Allowances

Monetary allowances are often provided to cover unsocial hours and expenses incurred by employees in connection with their work. Non-monetary allowances are also provided, particularly time-off in lieu for overtime working, although cash may be preferable to the employee. Although not technically an incentive, where these payments more than compensate for expenses and inconvenience, then an element of profit enters into the situation and they may represent some incentive to do the work. Living in large conurbations, particularly London, has often been considered justification for a special allowance to cover the higher costs of travel and living associated with these areas. Any incentive effect deriving from these allowances is very difficult to determine, and is probably secondary at best to the overall level of earnings.

New developments in incentive schemes

During the 1970s management, trade unions and employees became increasingly doubtful about the effectiveness of traditional payment by results, day work schemes and white-collar schemes. The incentive effect seemed difficult to maintain, and many schemes were contributing to escalating labour costs and inflation. The majority of organizations, interested in incentives, turned their attention in one of two directions.

In the case of schemes for production workers and indirect workers, new, or rather developed, techniques of work measurement were offered to provide better control of performance and to introduce more effective coverage of indirect work such as is found in maintenance departments and tool rooms. Examples of these schemes were Maynard's *Most*, the *Modac* (R) and *Logicon* approaches to improve the accuracy and consistency of measurement and control across a whole range of direct and indirect work. These methods involved the improved pre-determined motion time systems of measurement with the use of statistical analysis to verify the accuracy of the performance standards. In the case of *Modac* and *Logicon*, control was guaranteed to a tolerance of five per cent, in other words 95 per cent accuracy and coverage of work. In this way, the traditional problem of a high proportion of unmeasured work was to be solved. Alongside the improvements in measurement, developments in the reward payment system were designed to offer management a similar degree of control for labour costs.

There is no doubt that schemes such as those described above went some way towards improving control, incentive effect and costs associated with incentive schemes. Additionally, they offered a wider coverage of work, maintained consistency across that work and thus improved productivity on a wider front, while reducing disputes on comparability between measured and unmeasured employees. In the case of white-collar incentive schemes, the major development in the past 10 years has been the refinement of measurement for clerical and administrative work. Interest in these techniques has been limited, however, and completely overshadowed by the attractions of introducing a type of less direct incentive scheme to cover blue- and white-collar employees.

Value added incentive bonus schemes

An increasing number of companies now provide a value added statement alongside the more traditional profit and loss account and balance sheet. Value added is a measure of corporate performance in terms of wealth created over a period of time. This wealth derives from trading and operating not measured in terms of turnover, but in terms of sales minus the value of whatever has been 'bought in' to the process of making the product. If an item sells for £500, and the cost to the manufacturer of bought-in goods and services (raw materials, gas and electricity, for example) is £350, then the value added by this manufacturing company is £150. Therefore, Value Added = Sales minus Bought-in items over a period of time. The reason for considering value added as a basis for incentive schemes lies quite simply in the fact that it must reflect the performance of those involved in the work of the manufacturing unit, the employees in particular, along with those who provide capital. Because value added is a measure of output, it is possible to measure labour productivity merely by combining value added with labour characteristics in ratio form as follows:

(i)   Value Added per £1 of wages and salaries
(ii) Value Added per employee
(iii) Value Added per man-hour worked.

Value added can be measured in ratio form against the performance of any employee group if considered necessary. It is important to emphasize the raising of the ratio of value added to wages and salaries rather than the lowering of the ratio of wages and salaries to value added. In the former case, we are asking for an improvement in productivity. In the latter case, we are suggesting a reduction in real wages. The preferred ratio is value added per £1 of wages and salaries. Since value added and earnings are both measured in money terms, the ratio is less distorted by inflation than is the case with value added per employee and man-hour worked ratios.

The objectives of a value added incentive scheme have been claimed to be threefold:

(i)   to more closely involve employees in the achievement of corporate objectives;
(ii) to increase the earnings of employees by means of an equitable distribution of the increased wealth generated by the trading activities and operations of the company;
(iii) to improve the company's profitability and overall effectiveness in operations.

The requirements for the schemes are as follows:

(i)   the scheme should be self-financing;
(ii) people covered should be doing work with a common purpose;
(iii) the improvements in value added should be shared between the company and employees;
(iv) incentive bonus should be paid only when the improved value added is actually achieved;
(v)   profitability and return on capital should be maintained or preferably improved;
(vi) a monitoring scheme should be developed to ensure ongoing real movements in value added.

162

Employees can contribute to the process of increasing value added in the following ways:

(i)   increased sales by improving the quality and quantity of marketing; increasing selling activity, improved after sales service, product quality and delivery;
(ii)   improved utilization of company assets and reductions in costs;
(iii)   increasing the productivity of the manufacturing system;
(iv)   making better use of bought in items and thereby reducing costs.

The Method for a value added incentive scheme involves the calculation of a historical trend for movements in value added, and wages and salaries preferably over the immediate past five year period. The calculation for value added is Net Sales – Materials + Bought In Services + Depreciation. Employee costs can be calculated on the basis of wages and salaries, or indeed as total costs including benefits, national insurance contributions and the like. Normally wages and salaries are used. In working up the historical figures for value added, it is necessary to determine the following levels of distribution:

(i)   to employees
(ii)   to lenders as interest
(iii)   to government as profits tax
(iv)   to shareholders as dividends
(v)   to profit retention for investment and capital replacement.

A typical value added statement for this information is presented in table 6 on page 164. With wages and salaries and value added calculated for the five years it is possible to compute an index of value added for each year as follows:

$$\text{Wages and Salaries in 1977} = \text{£}24,500$$
$$\text{Value Added in 1977} = \text{£}265,000$$

$$\text{Index of Value Added 1977} = \frac{\text{£}24,500}{\text{£}265,000} = .0925 \times 100$$
$$= 9.25$$

The greater the ratio of value added to wages and salaries the lower is the index, and the more is being produced for a given employee cost.

On the basis of historical indices, management and employee representatives must agree a target index to be achieved in future years. Following from the example above, indices fluctuating between 9.00 and 9.75 over five years may be followed by a target index of say 9.00 to maintain the status quo or a target of 8.8 to provide substantial improvements. Readers might like to calculate the effect on their company financial performance of reducing the value added index by 2 per cent. In our example, £1 of value added is produced by 9 per cent wage and salary before and by 8.8 per cent after the introduction of the target in the bonus scheme.

Management must determine the share-out of any increase in value added. Schemes witnessed by this writer have provided for between 45 per cent and 60 per cent to employees and between 40 per cent and 55 per cent to the company in their early years, but tending to see the return to the company increasing towards 65 per cent in the third and fourth years. Companies normally calculate information for value added on a quarterly basis and the bonus is therefore paid every three months.

Table 6
Value added statement

	1977 £ %	1978 £ %	1979 £ %	1980 £ %	1981 £ %
Sales *less*					
bought in materials					
services					
depreciation					
less wages and salaries					
interest					
Value Added					
distribution					
employees					
interest on loans					
profits tax					
dividends					
profit retained					
Value Added per £1 of wages and salaries					

Experience with value added based incentive schemes
On paper, value added based incentives look very attractive and indicate considerable financial improvements for the company. But any approach to them should be cautious. Value added can easily fluctuate due to conditions outside the control of the firm including market conditions, national economic trends and inflation. Many employee representatives have not thoroughly understood the scheme and the

164

employee contribution to it. Managements have allowed the value added index and share for labour to become out of balance, with disastrous consequences for motivation and industrial relations when the proportions disadvantage the labour force, and unfortunate consequences for costs when labour's share is over generous. Employees have become disillusioned with value added schemes when management have used their existence in the company to counter normal wage claims. Finally, the payment of bonus at three monthly intervals works against a major principle of incentives. That bonus should be paid at short regular intervals in close proximity (in terms of time) to achieved performance.

Value Added, in the last analysis, is the aim of all businesses, and to adopt it as a basis for incentive schemes should be a means of ensuring a flourishing enterprise, and help companies away from the narrow and limited framework of 'effort bargaining'. This has not happened long-term in companies adopting value added incentives. The problem does not lie with the concept of value added but the approach adopted. For a reappraisal of value added and the incentive effect, the reader is referred to the following chapter.

Conclusions

The foregoing discussion reveals a continual struggle to find an incentive scheme for shop-floor employees which has real 'bite'. In the case of schemes for white-collar employees developments have been fewer. Salary progression and merit rating have to some extent held on, in the face of attempts to improve the popularity of clerical work measurement. In the move to value added schemes during the 1970s many companies turned away from any notion of the direct incentive for all employee groups. Although this has proved workable in the case of white-collar and managerial staffs, there is now a return to the direct incentive for manual workers, with value added continuing as some kind of background scheme. In reality the long term incentive effect has remained elusive with all types of schemes. In other words, management have not brought forward the employee performance levels which they have been paying for. It has also been unfortunate that PBR schemes and salary progression and merit schemes have neglected the wider issues of employee commitment to organization purpose. Yet incentive schemes remain popular, and the next chapter presents a review of the elements of design in incentive schemes, the failures of the past and a strategy offering some greater hope of success for the future.

Further reading on incentive schemes

Traditional payment by results

CURRIE R M, *Financial Incentives*. British Institute of Management 1969.

WHITMORE D A, *Work study and related management services.* Heinemann, various edns.

BROWN W, *Piecework abandoned—the effect of wage incentive schemes on managerial authority.* Heinemann, 1963.

Productivity agreements and day work schemes

McKENSIE R B *and* HUNTER L C, *Pay productivity and bargaining.* Macmillan, 1973.

NORTH D T B *and* BUCKINGHAM G L, *Productivity agreements and wage systems.* Gower Press 1969.

SMITH I G, *The measurement of productivity.* Gower Press 1974.

White-collar schemes

ARMSTRONG M *and* MURLIS H, *A handbook of salary administration.* Kogan Page, 1980.

Value added incentive schemes

MOORE J G, 'Added value as an index of Industrial effectiveness', in *Work Study and Management Services.* January 1973 Vol 17 No 1.

MORLEY M F, *The value added statement.* Gee and Co Ltd., 1978. Published for the Institute of Chartered Accountants of Scotland.

General

BOWEY A M *et al. Effects of incentive payment systems UK 1977–80.* Department of Employment research paper No 36. October 1982.

A management guide to incentive payment schemes. Institution of Production Engineers, 1982.

8
Incentive schemes:
effective design

It is possible to provide incentives for all employee groupings, although the schemes possess varying strengths of incentive effect. Financial incentives remain the most popular form of rewarding employee performance, increasing the effectiveness of work and controlling labour costs. They should also arouse interest amongst managers because of the potential contribution to company performance, although in practice this objective has been secondary to the more immediate earnings and worker performance issues. This is perhaps due to the lack of 'concrete' evidence or any positive effect these schemes may have on company performance. In the case of production work, scheme after scheme has been offered as the better alternative because of growing dissatisfaction with existing experiments. Thus, time rates and piecework schemes of various types have been followed by productivity agreements, day work schemes and value added with companies still searching for something which will maintain high levels of production in the long term. In this chapter some of the issues connected with the failure of incentive schemes are discussed. The required elements for effective schemes, particularly in production work, are considered and developed into an overall approach to employee performance, management control of labour costs and the links to organizational performance.

The failure of current initiatives

The failure of traditional PBR

Failing incentive schemes compound their own problems. Management lose confidence in controlling costs and performance, employees recognize this and take advantage of it in the belief that they are being left to make the best of a scheme which does not work. In these circumstances, employee behaviour may be directed at the pursuit of short term gains at the expense of the well-being of the scheme, and ultimately at the expense of the well-being of the enterprise. In this way, incentive schemes which could have contributed to the improvement of industrial performance have become major limitations.

Three causes of failure in incentive schemes stand out and these are as follows:

(i)   lack of a performance strategy to underpin the management of incentives
(ii) lack of effective controls for the pay and performance relationship
(iii) a reliance by management on the financial incentive alone with little or no attention to the design of work, equitable reward systems, and the behavioural dimensions of the work environment.

Management have therefore found themselves paying considerable sums of money without ensuring the presence of any performance 'return'.

With traditional PBR the situation has arisen from the difficulty in ensuring that all increases in pay arising from the operation of the scheme are offset by increased worker effort and resultant output. Precision in the measurement of effort and output has been lacking, and reductions in unit costs supposed to derive from increased worker effort have not been achieved. Consequently, wage drift and cost inflation have resulted.

In essence, traditional PBR has suffered from social, bargaining and technical pressures which have outpaced and outmoded this type of incentive scheme. The techniques of rating and time study, and indeed many other types of measurement, have not been enough on their own to raise productivity and in particular, they have not provided management with sufficiently effective controls for shop floor performance and labour costs. Additionally, traditional PBR has not allowed for attention to social issues such as worker frustration and the increasing post war problem of the shop floor challenge to management rights. Finally, a reliance on the incentive alone to ensure worker effort has created a tendency to ignore the issues of effective shop floor supervision and the need for a strategic approach to production and company performance.

The failure of modern PBR

The application of day work schemes, particularly to groups of workers or plant-wide, was initially seen as an improved alternative to traditional PBR. Experience proved otherwise, and this writer reported on the problems existing in two light engineering firms during 1976.[1] They had approximately 800 shop-floor employees involved in measured day work schemes introduced in the late sixties. In both firms there was one plant-wide consolidated earnings level. Production technology was of the mass production type.

The managements in both firms were agreed that the measured day work schemes had increased worker flexibility. The shop stewards agreed on this and accepted interchangeability as a necessary feature of improved work flow planning. On the other hand, the level of productivity in the firms had dropped by 15 to 20 per cent since the application of day work. It is difficult to define all the reasons for this, but management, shop stewards and employees agreed that individual operator performance could be improved to a level higher than attained in the best years of measured day work. To achieve this higher level of productivity, all parties in the two firms agreed that a direct financial incentive for the individual worker was necessary. The size of bonus discussed by managements and unions was between 10 and 15 per cent of the consolidated earnings payable in the plant-wide schemes. Measured day work thus needed to be accompanied by a significant pay increase during the process of implementation *and* during the process of elimination.

Productivity and pay were only part of the disenchantment with measured day work which existed in these two firms. Quality suffered considerably, with as much as a fifth of weekly output failing inspection. In both firms, all parties were convinced that quality would improve if responsibility for bonus earnings was returned to the individual worker. A significant cause of shop-floor disenchantment with measured day work was the inability of management to design and implement effective production planning. Thus, disputes over lack of materials and services were as prevalent in measured day work as in piecework.

Many of the problems associated with measured day work in the two firms came uncomfortably close to the problems associated with traditional PBR. As with piecework, low productivity was not the problem; it was rather a symptom of a management team being unable to ensure the appropriate production conditions which would allow measured day work to achieve the two main objectives of improved productivity and improved industrial relations. Unfortunately, both firms turned to a different type of incentive scheme instead of dealing with the root cause of the failure of the plant-wide schemes. Management, shop stewards and workers were convinced of the need to return to individual worker incentives. The absence of a strategy in the two firms, based on performance issues, left management without the means of identifying the need for and means of improving production management and work flow planning as a prerequisite to the effective operation of measured day work. One firm actually decided to return to piecework. Thus, 13 years after the publication of Wilfred Brown's book *Piecework Abandoned,*[2] two cases of measured day work abandoned had been discovered.

Measured day work has often been termed 'peaceful inefficiency' because disputes about incentive payments were reduced and so was the level of productivity. Lack of flexibility in earnings levels often left employees worse off than those paid by other methods, and in group and plant-wide schemes, good performers received the same size incentive payment as poor performers. By the mid-seventies there was a flight from measured day work, but there can be no doubt that those schemes were not given a reasonable chance to succeed. In their eagerness to buy in a ready-made packaged solution to the complex strategic and organizational problems of improving performance many companies failed to model day work to organizational contingencies and neglected to bolster its operation with improved production control and cost control.

The failure of indirect incentives

Documented evidence is hard to find on the subject of incentive schemes for white-collar staffs. There has been a lack of innovation in this area of the remuneration system, and it is therefore inescapable that merit schemes and salary progression schemes are outmoded by the current social, technical and economic factors affecting white-collar work. It is also reasonable to point out that the lack of effective measures of performance leads to the same problems of inadequate controls for performance and costs which have characterized manual schemes. Improving the efficiency and output of clerical and administrative employees remains a major task. The arrival of computer technology has already transformed the efficiency of such operations, but it is doubtful that this has been matched by some effective measure of employee contributions to efficiency.

The incentive effect in schemes for manual production workers has always been greater than in schemes for indirect production workers and white-collar staffs, at least in the short term. The underlying reasons for this are the more apparent nature of the results of production tasks, the comparative ease of measuring production worker performance and the direct link between performance and pay which can be readily understood by employees. Experience shows that the ability to measure results, and the provision of feedback to the employee of a clear picture of what is being rewarded, can result in some change in employee motivation, although it must be repeated that evidence on the long term maintenance of high levels of motivation is somewhat scarce. The same effect on motivation can be seen in management level bonus schemes where again measurement is more effective.

Without such feedback it is reasonable to assume that indirect schemes provide a weak impetus to employee motivation. Salary progression, merit rating, value added and the like are probably not incentives at all. Rather they are goodwill payments ('enabling payments' may be better terms to describe them), and as such they could be a useful means of obtaining employee co-operation on the introduction of the changes, and the methods necessary to underpin an incentive payment based on detailed measurement. Such a measurement based approach may be a radical departure for many indirect groups and will probably be resisted. The enabling payments are, of course, offered to overcome such resistance.

Measurement for indirect manual work and white-collar work may be in its infancy, but it offers the only real hope of injecting an incentive effect into such operations and of providing commonality and comparability across remuneration structures for all categories of work excepting management. In this last case, financial incentives should be linked to measurable corporate performance; an issue which will be returned to later.

The failure of value added

There is no doubt that in the vacuum created by the failure of traditional incentive schemes, management turned their attention away from work measurement to the procedures of the accountant in order to create an incentive scheme for the eighties. Value added schemes have enjoyed a chequered career in British industry, and two particular difficulties have inhibited the effective operation of these schemes. The calculation of bonus on the basis of a relationship between value added and labour costs takes some time. Six weeks is the minimum period witnessed by this writer, and three months is common. The data simply takes this long to collect and analyse. Therefore, value added schemes break the cardinal rule of all incentive schemes: *that payment of bonus should be made close in time to the achieved performance level, in other words, a 'Short Bounce Period'.* A second problem can be described as the 'nil incentive'. Because payment of bonus is at regular intervals and divorced in time from worker performance, it becomes an expected part of the pay packet; extra effort and increased output are not perceived by the employee as part of the 'value added' package. Faced with this situation many managements have been forced to introduce or reintroduce a weekly productivity based incentive payment to maintain output. Such managements are thus trapped with the two costs of value added and traditional PBR, with no real confidence that either scheme is improving productivity.

Where value added is introduced to replace a more traditional productivity based scheme the problems described above will soon become apparent. Additionally, management encounter considerable resistance from employee representatives when they attempt to separate out inflation-caused increases in the ratio of value added to wages and salaries. In this connection the indexing of value added has not provided a long term solution, and even if they accept indexing, employees increasingly demand some reflection of price inflation in their bonus, if only through the calculation of a new index base-line. Indeed many trade unionists see such indexing as a threat to their bargaining rights in respect of the employees' remuneration.

In firms with no history of incentive schemes, value added has provided some benefits particularly in clearing the decks to new agreements on such items as manning, flexibility and overtime. Whether productivity increases have occurred and been sustained in the longrun is doubtful.

For white collar workers, value added may be deemed appropriate, particularly where management do not feel inclined to introduce some direct measurement of work, yet wish to give staff something extra which restores some differential with shop-floor pay levels. That such a payment will act as an incentive is again debatable, and management may conclude that the results do not justify the cost of the scheme.

The need for new thinking

The concept of value added is not in dispute, indeed it must be an objective for all productivity based payment schemes, but using value added as a prerequisite to increased productivity has been a mistake in too many organizations. The question remains of how to design an effective incentive scheme which directly rewards worker performance, increases productivity and improves the firm's overall performance. In other words, how to design a scheme which uses an incentive based on employee performance as a prerequisite to the improvement of value added.

In the first instance, these improvements require an assessment of managerial responsibilities and attitudes. Senior management often fail to ensure that efforts to increase productivity are the responsibility of line managers, and all too often leave such attempts to the personnel or management services departments, whose lack of line authority leaves them in the invidious position of directing the work of line managers. Productivity involves all resources for which line management in the production function should have sole responsibility. This should be coupled with senior management support and commitment to improved productivity, and the means of achieving it. Only top management can 'tune' productivity to corporate objectives; co-ordinate the separate efforts of line and specialist managers, and finally, and most importantly, set a management style that results in all managers and employees wanting to achieve compatible objectives, within a performance orientated strategy. In these terms, the management of productivity and pay is a top management function.

As in all matters concerning company performance, management attitudes are the prerequisite to change and results. Past social changes coupled with a rising level of education attainment among work-forces have outmoded traditional and respected approaches to the management of the human resource. Thus the tools of measuring and managing the performance of production systems and people have been outmoded. In particular, the industrial engineers' methods of work measurement have become increasingly abused and mis-applied in the more complex mixes of technology and people expectation and behaviour which are the industrial concerns of the present day. Many personnel managers and industrial engineers are indeed aware of these problems, but their line management colleagues often allow no opportunity to apply new ideas. In these circumstances, industrial engineering and the management of incentives has become irrelevant to, and has 'stalled' within, the process of ensuring corporate well-being. In the design and operation of incentive schemes, more than in any other aspect of remuneration, management should recognize the appropriateness of a strategic approach which links decisions on pay to corporate requirements for performance. The elements of such an approach to incentive schemes can be synthesized from the lessons deriving from past failures. Emphasis is placed on shop-floor conditions for this discussion.

Elements in an ideal incentive payment plan

Problems with incentive systems of all types suggest that success requires the following objectives:

(i) low installation costs
(ii) low running costs

(iii) containment of all costs by financial improvements in organization performance so that the scheme is at least self-financing
(iv) performance standards and payment levels to be mutually agreed by management and employees
(v) earnings stability for employees
(vi) choice of earnings levels for employees
(vii) genuine and measurable improvements in productivity
(viii) regular audit and update of procedures for performance and pay
(ix) monitoring the effectiveness in the management of the scheme.

The achievement of these objectives will be difficult and will take time, but they should be realizable if the organization can introduce the following:

(i) low cost work measurement to cover a high proportion of direct and indirect work
(ii) motivating payment structures
(iii) employee dividends based on value added.

These three provisions are considered essential to a performance orientated remuneration strategy, and are discussed in some detail below.

Work measurement

Incentive schemes are obviously concerned with the proceeds or shares of improved performance and shares of any value cannot be negotiated without a 'non-subjective' definition of size. This involves measurement whether in terms of value added or unit cost, or physical units produced, or any other unit of count. It is, therefore, useful to reassess the role of work measurement in measuring productivity as a basis for payment systems.

The tasks of work measurement in incentive schemes can be defined as follows:

(i) to provide improved control data, and management control of shop-floor performance
(ii) work standards should be indisputable and based on a consistent measure of the maximum amount of work
(iii) the measurement method and work values should gain acceptance on the shop-floor by being fair and equitable bases on which to calculate pay and performance
(iv) management should be provided with 'hard' measured improvements in productivity

(v)   the methods used should be cost effective, saving the company more money than the method costs—a situation not always found in firms with industrial engineering departments

(vi) finally, work measurement should get to grips with the excessive amounts of unmeasured work in British industry, particularly in tool rooms, maintenance departments and offices.

Low cost work measurement systems, which can meet these requirements have been proven in a wide range of industries around the world during the last two decades. In working closely with the development of these systems it has been possible to see their original application to highly variable work situations expanded to areas of work where more traditional techniques would have been used, and where variable operator performance and the resultant wage drift are out of control. The main features of such systems, which will measure most areas of work are:

(i)   the traditional work study approach to defining 'elements' is replaced by definitions of 'tasks' or 'activities'. *These tasks are defined in the language of the skill* and not the language of work study. Thus the system is more acceptable to employees because it is in their language

(ii) this method of defining tasks reduces the volume of work study data required. Thus labour standards can be applied quickly even in highly 'unpredictable' work situations

(iii) rapid application of work standards considerably reduces the time and therefore the costs associated with the measurement. Additionally, installation costs are a once only affair, and running costs are reduced through a simplified management information system

(iv) technical soundness can be derived from the provision of work standards for 90 per cent to 95 per cent of all work—direct and indirect.

Effective and consistent work measurement
Work values are normally expressed in standard hours, and if we find a job with, say, 1.2 standard hours, and ask the operator how often the job is finished in that time, his reply will usually be '. . . hardly ever'. In the harsh reality of the shop-floor environment, any job which proves difficult will result in pressures being placed on the work study engineer to allow more time, and thus more money for the job. In this way 'wage drift' becomes endemic to incentive schemes because the time and pay for jobs moves away from the levels orginally specified for the PBR

scheme. We need to be clear how much more difficult is difficult, and how much extra time should be allowed. How can we measure something which is more or less difficult than the average?

The answer to this question is that work measurement should measure the variability in work and performance which so often gives rise to disputes about times and wage drift, so that management can obtain control of, and not eliminate it. A first step to the control of variability would be a greater reliance on predetermined motion time systems, such as methods time measurement, which replace the inconsistency of rate fixer determined *ad hoc* rating with a consistency of rating at a predetermined level of performance on the British standard scale (normally in the region of 83). The work study data can then be processed using statistical sampling techniques to check the accuracy of the times derived from the measurement exercise and to, therefore, offer some confidence (or even guarantee) to management that the resultant work values or performance standards are sufficient to allow management to control variability to an accuracy of ±5 per cent.

Such a degree of accuracy is much more realistic than is the case with traditional and modern PBR schemes which attempt to pay each individual performance point, on the British standard scale, by one payment point or unit. This 100 per cent accuracy is impossible to achieve with any work measurement technique. A tolerance of ±5 per cent may not be absolute accuracy, but it offers something for incentive schemes which is essential to the control of pay and performance: *consistency in the work values as a basis for consistency in pay.* This consistency advantage derives from the fact that while 100 per cent accuracy may not be consistently achievable, a ±5 per cent tolerance is realistic and viable in the workplace setting. With the knowledge that the control of work is to within this tolerance management can turn their attention to the design of the incentive payment structure.

Incentive pay structure design

There are five basic requirements to be met if pay is to be a motivator:

(i) pay should meet the 'instrumental' expectations of workers. Thus pay levels should be competitive in the local labour market

(ii) reward should equate to the individual's personal evaluation of his work effort and it should stand comparison with pay for similar work and effort elsewhere, both within and outside the organization. Relative pay motivates, not total pay

(iii) pay should be influenced by worker discretion. Paying the same bonuses to everyone will demotivate workers and depress performance. The low performers, high performers and average performers should be rewarded accordingly to maximize motivation

(iv) pay should be based on equal earnings opportunities. In this way the incentive scheme can maximize discretion, be seen to be fair, and improve worker motivation and performance. Dissatisfaction and comparability problems will be minimized if all workers have the *same opportunity* to perform and earn bonus

(v) bonus should be paid close to the achieved performance.

To meet these requirements for incentive payments in turn requires some improved but realistic degree of accuracy in determining pay and an appropriate pay structure.

Calculating pay

If management are often unaware of the accuracy of the data on which work values are determined, they must be unaware of the accuracy of the data on which employees are paid. If work values can be improved to a degree of accuracy of ±5 per cent then it should be possible to determine pay to ±5 per cent.

With the traditional approach of 'payment point based on performance point' as used traditionally in PBR schemes, employee pay can vary because of falls in performance which may well not be the employees' fault (*see* the section of 'Premium pay plan' in chapter 7 for evidence on causes of poor operator performance). Furthermore, as discussed in the preceding section, this degree of 100 per cent accuracy is not attainable in the determination of performance and is therefore not practical for determining pay.

If total accuracy is not possible in the attempt to calculate payment levels then, as with the measurement exercise, it becomes preferable to aim for some consistency in a range or tolerance for pay again at ± 5 per cent. For example, with the traditional point by point scheme a performance of 96 will be paid £96, 97 is £97 and so on to £105 for a British standard scale performance of 105. Instead it may be realistic to pay one pay level (say £95) for a performance range of 96 to 105. (The figures used assume consolidated payments based on standard hours for one week.)

With pay for a performance range, based on a ± 5 per cent tolerance, the pay period tolerances for performance variations are known to ±5 per cent. In other words performance variations have now been accommodated in the play calculations exercise. How many people reading these words know the pay period tolerances of their organizations performance standards, and how many would benefit by controlling them at ±5 per cent?

It must be emphasized that this degree of control can only be achieved if it is based on the same degree of consistent control in determining performance standards. The two go hand in hand in the pay performance calculation.

The stepped pay band structure

The stepped pay band structure allows the operator to choose his own rate of working (in other words which performance range he wishes to slot into) and provides for stabilized earnings. Additionally, the administration of stepped pay band structures has proved simpler in terms of bonus calculation which in turn can lead to reduced clerical costs.

The stepped pay band structure would normally include no less than three and no more than five steps. Four steps are presented below, with the pay level determined at the mid-point of the range.

performance range	contribution level	pay level
75–85	learning	80
86–95	intermediate	90
96–105	standard	100
106–115	super	110

The employee is allowed to choose his own step and is checked for a period of four weeks to ensure that he maintains performance. Thereafter a random 10 per cent weekly check on performance is carried out. Simple and workable rules govern the movement of employees up and down the steps with a four week delay in each direction. This arrangement regularly proves acceptable in practice.

In this way, the stepped structure provides consistency of earnings with a choice of earnings level, and should help control wage drift and reduce the opportunities for disputes about performance standards and pay.

The alternative to the stepped pay band is the straight line proportional pay structure which has traditionally been very popular. As discussed in the fore-going section, this approach assumes that the worker can be paid a unit of payment for each point of performance improvement, and this is shown in diagrammatic form in figure 17.

178

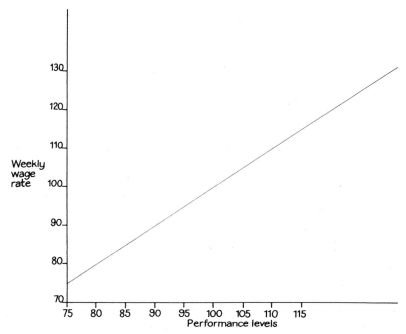

Figure 17
Straight line proportional pay scheme

The weekly wage rate is usually for all hours worked, excluding overtime, and therefore pay is for standard hours. At a performance level of 85 and weekly hours of 40, the operator is paid £85 for 40 hours × 85 = 3400 standard hours. At a performance of 90, the operator is paid at £90 per week, at 91 he is paid £91, and so on.

There are two major drawbacks to the use of this straight line proportional approach to determining pay:

(i) work measurement is not accurate enough to guarantee that a one point improvement in performance is actually being achieved

(ii) each operator has his or her own pay level which contributes to complexity and provides too many opportunities for disputes about comparability issues.

The stepped pay band approach can avoid these problems if payments are based on a tolerance of ±5 per cent of the performance level being paid for, and thus drastically reduces the number of pay levels and simplifies the pay structure. Figure 18 on page 180 presents the stepped pay band structure in diagram form.

179

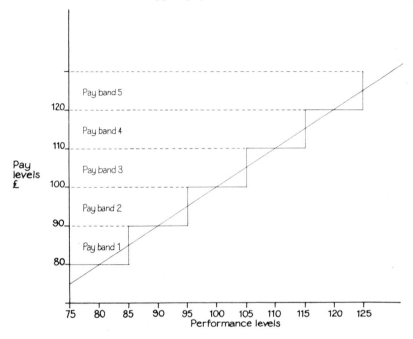

Figure 18
The stepped pay band structure

In figure 18 the idea of pay bands in steps can be appreciated. Pay band 1 would be provided for training. Instead of £1 increments, we now have one pay level for a 10 point range of employee performance as follows:

Pay band 1 pays £80 for 75 to 85 performance
Pay band 2 pays £90 for 86 to 95 performance
Pay band 3 pays £100 for 96 to 105 performance
Pay band 4 pays £110 for 106 to 115 performance
Pay band 5 pays £120 for 116 to 125 performance.

In reality, however, the pay bands can be determined differently from this. The bottom point or top point could be used, depending on what can be negotiated and what is considered viable.

Employees can move to a higher or lower pay band to reflect their individual performance. This helps to strengthen managerial control of labour costs while directly rewarding individual contributions to production.

The effect of the stepped pay band structure in simplifying pay structures is revealed by a comparison of tables 7 and 8 on pages 181 and

182. The figures are taken from an actual pay structure current at April 1983 in an engineering firm. Five pay bands are applied to each grade, covering unskilled, semi-skilled, skilled, foremen and inspector employee groupings. In the example, the performance range has been extended from a high of 120 to a new high of 125. Experience has shown that 125 is a realistic level of attainment, but beyond this level it is doubtful that worker performance alone is being recorded and rewarded. The 75 to 85 range is for training.

Table 7
Pay structure determined by straight line proportional approach

Pay and perform- ance index	GRADE					
	I Gross pay per 39 hrs ₤	II Gross pay per 39 hrs ₤	III Gross pay per 39 hrs ₤	IV Gross pay per 39 hrs ₤	V Gross pay per 39 hrs ₤	VI Gross pay per 39 hrs ₤
75	96.98	86.05	82.15	79.07	72.66	63.77
76	97.88	86.89	82.95	79.85	73.14	64.33
77	98.78	87.72	83.75	80.62	73.62	64.89
78	99.68	88.56	84.55	81.40	74.10	65.45
79	100.58	89.39	85.35	82.17	74.58	66.01
80	101.48	90.23	86.15	82.95	75.06	66.57
81	102.38	91.06	86.95	83.72	75.54	67.13
82	103.28	91.90	87.75	84.50	76.02	67.69
83	104.18	92.73	88.55	85.27	76.50	68.25
84	105.08	93.57	89.35	86.05	76.98	68.81
85	105.98	94.40	90.15	86.82	77.46	69.37
86	106.88	95.24	90.95	87.60	77.94	69.93
87	107.78	96.07	91.75	88.37	78.42	70.49
88	108.68	96.91	92.55	89.15	78.90	71.05
89	109.58	97.74	93.35	89.92	79.38	71.61
90	110.48	98.58	94.15	90.70	79.86	72.17
91	111.38	99.41	94.95	91.47	80.34	72.73
92	112.28	100.25	95.75	92.25	80.82	73.29
93	113.18	101.08	96.55	93.02	81.30	73.85
94	114.08	101.92	97.35	93.80	81.78	74.41
95	114.98	102.75	98.15	94.57	82.26	74.97
96	115.88	103.59	98.95	95.35	82.74	75.53
97	116.78	104.42	99.75	96.12	83.22	76.09
98	117.68	105.26	100.55	96.90	83.70	76.65
99	118.58	106.09	101.35	97.67	84.18	77.21
100	119.48	106.93	102.15	98.45	84.66	77.77
101	120.38	107.76	102.95	99.22	85.14	78.33
102	121.28	108.60	103.75	100.00	85.62	78.89
103	122.18	109.43	104.55	100.77	86.10	79.45
104	123.08	110.27	105.35	101.55	86.58	80.01

	GRADE					
	I	II	III	IV	V	VI
Pay and perform-ance index	Gross pay per 39 hrs £	Gross pay per 39 hrs £	Gross pay per 39 hrs £	Gross pay per 39 hrs £	Gross pay per 39 hrs £	Gross pay per 39 hrs £
105	123.98	111.10	106.15	102.32	87.06	80.57
106	124.88	111.94	106.95	103.10	87.54	81.13
107	125.78	112.77	107.75	103.87	88.02	81.69
108	126.68	113.61	108.55	104.65	88.50	82.25
109	127.58	114.44	109.35	105.42	88.98	82.81
110	128.48	115.28	110.15	106.20	89.46	83.37
111	129.38	116.11	110.95	106.97	89.94	83.93
112	130.28	116.95	111.75	107.75	90.42	84.49
113	131.18	117.78	112.55	108.52	90.90	85.05
114	132.08	118.62	113.35	109.30	91.38	85.61
115	132.98	119.45	114.15	110.07	91.86	86.17
116	133.88	120.29	114.95	110.85	92.34	86.73
117	134.78	121.12	115.75	111.62	92.82	87.29
118	135.68	121.96	116.55	112.40	93.30	87.85
119	136.58	122.79	117.35	113.17	93.78	88.41
120	137.48	123.63	118.15	113.95	94.26	88.97

Table 8
Pay structure determined by stepped pay bands

	GRADE					
	I	II	III	IV	V	VI
Pay and perform-ance index	Gross pay per 39hrs £	Gross pay per 39hrs £	Gross pay per 39hrs £	Gross pay per 39hrs £	Gross pay per 39hrs £	Gross pay per 39hrs £
75–85	101.48	90.23	86.15	82.95	75.06	66.57
86–95	110.48	98.58	94.15	90.70	79.86	72.17
96–105	119.48	106.93	102.15	98.45	84.66	77.77
106–115	128.48	115.28	110.15	106.20	89.46	83.37
116–125	137.48	123.63	118.15	113.95	94.26	88.97

If companies wish to allow for performance levels below 75 and above 125, for whatever reason, there is no problem and the number of bands is merely increased. In warehouses, and in operations with very low performance levels, for example, it has been useful to introduce a 65 to 75 performance based pay band. Where the machine influence in work cycles has pushed performance beyond 125, it has been possible to introduce a 126 to 135 performance based pay band. Care is needed in introducing such high bands since many workers may exert pressure to get into it, a problem which is worthy of further attention.

Dealing with drift

One question which is frequently raised in connection with the use of pay bands concerns the tendency for employee performance to move to and stay in the highest band, the end result being that the majority of employees are clustered in this band. This problem is really the same as that which arises with all incentive schemes when operator performance 'creeps' upwards. Usually managerial worries about this phenomenon are coupled with a growing awareness that perhaps recorded measurements of performance are higher than actual performance.

The answer to questions about clustering can be found in the structural issues relevant to operator performance, including work methods and equipment and performance controls. A weakness of all incentive schemes is the lack of attention given to methods before measurement is applied. Too often, ineffective methods determine mediocre levels of performance, and then as the scheme is applied operators learn short cuts and methods which improve their recorded performance but not their actual improvement. Indeed, worker defined improvements in methods should be rewarded, but not in the chaotic way of allowing people to drift upwards to the highest band. For dealing with these methods improvements the reader is referred to the section 'employee dividends and value added' on page 187.

Jointly agreed and effective controls on performance and pay are also needed to stop this drift. Additionally, foremen need to be trained specifically in the means of managing performance close in to the standards determined for the scheme. Failure to provide this degree of control in the past has created a situation where many pay systems have been developed to cover the inability of work measurement (or lack of it) to achieve control of work where variability of performance is endemic, or to cover management's inability to control their company's industrial relations. Thus we end up in the classical situation of management not knowing what they are paying for.

In dealing with this situation, it is necessary to calculate 'mean' performance levels for all jobs. Thus any deviation from the mean can then be readily identified. Management at least know what is happening and can quickly investigate, and if necessary respond to the causes. According to the circumstances, they can attend to the conditions in the work environment which are causing poor or improved operator performance or move him/her to a lower or higher pay band, whichever is appropriate.

Improved control of pay

It is appropriate to emphasize that paying one level of remuneration for

183

a range of performance offers more control of pay than has traditionally been the case. Indeed, the determination of pay to plus or minus 5 points of a given performance level, provides a degree of control over pay unheard of in much of British industry. Perhaps the reader would like to calculate the results in his company of obtaining this degree of control and simultaneously simplifying remuneration structures. Despite the range for performance and the containment of variability in performance, some deviation in operator performance will remain a problem and require further measures.

Variable operator performance

It is often the case with shop-floor incentive schemes that any deviations from targeted performance levels actually go undetected. When they are detected management usually decide to classify such work as unmeasured or special category work, or development work. Payment is usually made on the basis of average earnings, regardless of the level of achieved performance. These average earnings payments have become a 'malignant' component of payment systems, and nobody is really sure what is being paid for. The underlying cause of the situation is uncontrolled variability in actual operator performance because management have failed to adopt the following approach.

Where operator performance falls off then his performance index will fall, and usually this happens because of non-productive work. Time spent producing is of course paid at the performance level or index achieved, but non-productive time should be paid at normal, or lowest PI of 75. If the rules of the incentive scheme are jointly agreed clear and fair this state of affairs should be possible, and unmeasured work should be minimized, and rigidly controlled with closely monitored clocking on and off the job. The pay at performance index 75 should be low enough to pressure the operator to quickly finish unmeasured work and return to measured work with an incentive.

Some situations arise, however, where operator performance inevitably deviates from the mean and such deviation is acceptable because of the work mix or work load which are unpredictable. The traditional answer to this problem has been to extend the pay period from one week to say four to smooth out operator performances, but direct operatives usually reject this approach because pay is too divorced in time from achievement.

Examples of this problem work are the Gas Board engineers who can spend from 30 minutes to a whole week on a gas escape; or a production line where 'one offs' are introduced in the interests of customer service; or an assembly operation coping with variable quality of component items. Ideally we should be able to measure such work, but we will still be left with unpredictable operator performance and the problem of what to do about his pay.

The solution to the problem lies in a process known as 'exponential smoothing' or in simpler terms the '*Trend Pay Performance Index*'. It is the case that as managers we prefer to decide on the basis of trends rather than individual incidents in all aspects of the managerial task.

Smoothing the trend of performance

The smoothing of variations in operator performance has the effect of spreading all variations over a period of time. The overall results prove to be accurate, are acceptable to employees, are easy to calculate and maintain and are capable of providing for stability in earnings. One problem which needs to be understood by all parties is that the greater the smoothing of variations in performance, the more difficult it becomes for the employee to raise his earnings level after suffering a fall due to a detected lowering of performance which is defined as operator caused. Once earnings go down, attempts to improve performance will be so smoothed out that a passage of some time will be required before earnings can go up again. The steps in this smoothing exercise are as follows:

(i) decide the length of time needed to smooth out variations to reduce them to plus or minus 5 points of the mean performance level. As a guide, variations of ±10 per cent require two to three weeks; over 50 per cent require 10 weeks. 4 weeks is the period most commonly used

(ii) calculate an average pay and performance index (PPI) over a period which is longer than that determined for the smoothing. This becomes the starting trend PPI

(iii) the percentage weighting of the PPI's is determined on the basis of the following calculation:

$$\text{Smoothing Period} = 1 + \frac{\% \text{ Last Trend PPI}}{\% \text{ Current Weeks PPI}}$$

$$\therefore 4 \text{ weeks} = 1 + \frac{3}{1} \text{ or } \frac{75}{25}$$

The higher figure (75) is used as a percentage for last week's PPI and 25 for the current weeks PPI.

(iv) Example:
Let us take the case of an operator whose weekly performance index varies as follows:
Trend before smoothing period at 100

1st week of smoothing period at 80
2nd week of smoothing period at 100
3rd week of smoothing period at 140
4th week of smoothing period at 75.

We will assume that the last trend is weighted at 75 per cent and current PI at 25 per cent. Therefore pay is calculated as follows:

1st week

$$100 \times .75 = 75.00$$
$$80 \times .25 = \underline{20.00}$$

New smoothed PI $= \underline{95.00}$

Therefore pay in week 1 is at 95 PI

2nd week

$$95 \times .75 = 71.25$$
$$100 \times .25 = \underline{25.00}$$

New smoothed PI $= \underline{96.25}$

Therefore pay in week 2 is at 96.25 (say 96) PI

3rd week

$$96 \times .75 = 72.00$$
$$140 \times .25 = \underline{35.00}$$

New smoothed PI $= \underline{107.77}$

Therefore pay in week 3 is at 107 PI

4th week

$$107 \times .75 = 80.25$$
$$75 \times .25 = \underline{18.75}$$

New smoothed PI $= \underline{99.00}$

Therefore pay in week 4 is at 99 PI

This example of smoothing is presented in graph form in figure 19 on page 187. These PPIs may have to be treated outside the stepped payband structure, although there is no reason why the smoothed trend PPIs should not be slotted into the bands and paid at the normal rate for the band. It is usual for the minimum paid in this approach to be 75 PI. The maximum needs to be set above the normal ceiling (say by 5 points) to allow the operator the opportunity to attain the ceiling or highest pay band. In this way, operator induced performance variations are monitored and paid appropriately and quickly. Costs are controlled and performance can be motivated upwards by the response to any deterioration.

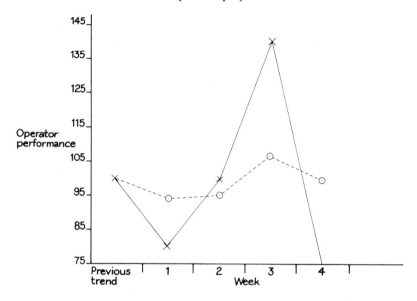

Figure 19
Graph to show the effect of exponential smoothing on highly
variable operator performance

Key: ✗——— Operator performance before smoothing
     ○------ Operator performance after smoothing

Employee dividends and value added

Through the more effective control of the pay and performance
relationship, management are presented with an opportunity to cease
fire-fighting measurement problems and concentrate on methods
improvements to further reduce costs. This will require the co-
operation of employees to accept the tightening of time standards
brought about by such improvements. More important is the
requirement for management to tap the knowledge of employees. This
will cost money. As discussed earlier, employees often keep method
improvements to themselves to enhance earnings, which behaviour
contributes to wage drift and inflation. Thus management make
'uncontrolled' payments in the form of artificially high pay performance.

An employee dividend plan, which is presented in figure 20 on page
189 can help create improvements in productivity on the basis of first
creating 'value added', through methods changes, and then sharing it
out equitably. Thus management and employees can share productivity

187

savings on a 50/50 basis. Savings could be accumulated in the first 12 month period and paid out during the subsequent 12 month period in whatever quantities and at whatever intervals are deemed to be appropriate. In the second and subsequent years of the pay plan, *all savings* can be used to maintain a dynamic element in remuneration policy. The financing of pay-outs to employees is now based on method improvements from employees *and* the industrial engineering department *and* from capital expenditure by management.

Further savings within the value added plan could be derived from the auditing and up-dating of work standards or values annually. This auditing and up-dating of the basic elements of the dividend plan would allow its continuing application, thus providing more method and capital created improvements in productivity, and a longer lasting and more financially sound means of generating value added to be shared by employees, shareholders and the customers.

The role of participation

The contribution of effective work measurement to productivity and the development of method improvements may be facilitated by shop-floor or task participation which can help to tap the employees' knowledge of work. Through task participation, employees have an opportunity to realize their 'hoped for prerogative' of influencing the work environment, and can be involved in the work of production rather than the deployment and maintenance of restrictive practices. The suggestion here is to limit participation to the management 'style' used to administer the productivity based incentive scheme. This would involve employees in carrying out work measurement, applying performance standards and control data, and in the every day administration of the scheme including grievance procedures and the design and introduction of modifications.

Indirect staff and incentives

The emphasis of the foregoing has been on shop-floor conditions, and in particular on schemes for direct or production workers. It is in this area that the incentive has its most obvious application, and much of the discussion in this chapter has revealed the many problems which need to be solved. Indeed, it is reasonable to suggest that incentive schemes for indirect categories of staff should wait until production schemes are perfected.

The principles of effective control of pay and performance also discussed in this chapter are as important for indirect schemes as they are for direct schemes. The use of log-normal techniques and category

Figure 20
The sharing of value added

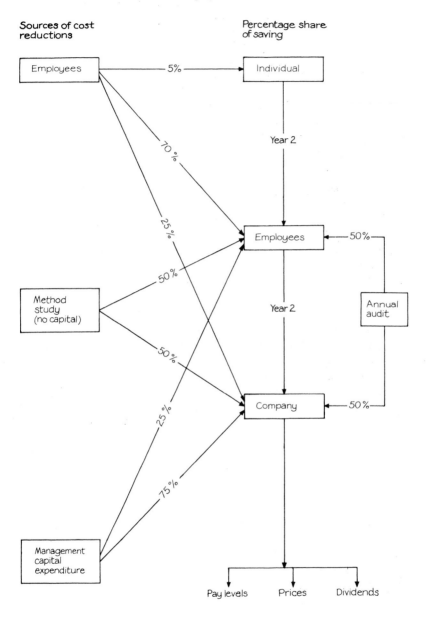

Sources of cost reductions

Percentage share of saving

Employees ——— 5% ——→ Individual

70 %

25 %

Year 2

Employees ←—— 50%

50%

Method study (no capital)

Year 2

Annual audit

50%

25 %

Company ←—— 50%

75 %

Management capital expenditure

Pay levels   Prices   Dividends

estimating for determining performance levels in maintenance and tool room work hold out the hope of providing adequately accurate standards to support a pay system which actually rewards achieved and verifiable performance. Clerical work measurement such as the Israeli Productivity Institute System and the British Rail Clerical Work Measurement System, may offer similar hope, although measurement may be based on elements rather different in nature to those found in measurement techniques for manual work. Alternatively, value added may be the viable basis of clerical and administrative schemes designed to provide some kind of incentive effect, although that effect will be substantially different in nature from the incentive effects on the shop-floor.

Management incentives

The types of scheme available for management were discussed in chapter 7 (pages 139–66) and the provision of some bonus seems to be the preferred method. Many companies have found profit sharing or value added to be acceptable bases for determining the size of bonus. Alternatively, managerial bonuses can be in kind, such as a more expensive company car.

There is evidence that interest in incentive schemes for top executives is currently growing, with cash bonus and share option schemes at the forefront in terms of popularity.[3] The reductions in higher marginal tax rates in the 1979 budget has doubtless given impetus to this popularity, particularly in the case of cash incentives. In a 1982 survey of 56 companies half were involved in some form of cash or share based incentive scheme for executives, but the majority of schemes were in the early stages of operation and thus it was too soon to conclude on the effectiveness of the schemes in terms of meeting the objectives laid down for them. Certainly the limited evidence collected suggested that companies were generally satisfied with the scheme and stressed an acceptance by management of the link between achievement and reward.[4]

A difficulty with management incentive schemes arises with the setting of targets and the appropriate measures. Executives should be involved in the process of determining targets jointly with their superiors who will then monitor and evaluate performance. In this connection some form of performance improvement plan within set time limits (containing objectives relevant to managerial and corporate performance) may be useful. Management by Objectives may provide the basis for improvement plans for all management levels, and this method may be worthy of a fresh inspection by companies anxious to improve the order of results achieved by their middle and senior managers in particular. One approach to operationalizing Management by Objectives has been provided by Mali who emphasizes the productivity issue by evaluating management decisions and actions in terms of the relationship between management performance and expenditure by the manager on resources; a relationship which is regarded by Mali as the essence of productivity.[5] Thus Mali recommends that management performance should be measured in terms of several dimensions: what is achieved: the manager's effectiveness in achieving objectives (such as problem solving ability, organizing ability): the use of resources (time, supplies, money and people): the personal characteristics of the manager.[6] Unfortunately, Mali does not translate this evaluation of managerial performance into some kind of incentive scheme. Indeed management by objectives schemes are rarely used as a basis for determining executive pay. As with performance appraisal schemes, there seems to be a general reluctance to associate the scheme with matters of remuneration. This attitude should change if managerial motivation is to be influenced by financial incentives.

Clearly the prerequisite to determining objectives and providing greater motivation for managers is an analysis of company performance and the synthesis of a company profit improvement plan. The reward can usefully take the form of cash based on the improvement of value added, with this reward linked to individual manager contributions to the level of company profitability. Close analysis of small improvements achieved by management actions in the areas of stock turnover, purchasing spend, employee efficiency, volume and prices and the resultant large increases in company profitability would prompt many organizations to introduce the management incentive scheme, and ensure a quality of management capable of achieving the results. Improvements at fractions of one percentage point in many areas of managerial activity can improve profitability by 20 per cent or more when their effect is accumulated.

Administering cash executive incentives

In the case of cash bonuses a decision will have to be made on whether to make the bonus pensionable, when to admit people to the scheme, what to do about bonus for people who leave the company before payment is made and when to make payment. Usually companies pay executive bonuses on an annual basis which smoothes out fluctuations to enable the payments to be pensionable. It is useful to admit people to the scheme at the beginning of the financial year no matter when they joined the company, and evidence suggests that many companies still pay bonus to leavers.

The design of the executive incentive scheme may be on the basis of a bonus fund scheme or an individual or direct scheme (*see* chapter 7 on page 152). The two examples below are presented to show the methods of calculation appropriate to these two approaches to the provision of cash bonuses to executives.[7]

Example 1
Executive cash incentives calculated by the bonus fund method

A proportion of the profits is normally set aside in a bonus pool which is allocated to each executive within the scheme as a percentage of salary as follows:

Capital employed	£50,000K
Profit before tax	£11,000K
Target return on capital of 20%	£10,000K
Additional profit generated by the achievement of the ROC target	£1,000K
Executives 1% pool	£10K
Total salary bill for executive group	£150K

$$\text{Bonus calculation is } \frac{1\% \text{ pool}}{\text{Total salary bill}} \quad \frac{£10\text{K}}{£150\text{K}} \quad = 6.66$$

Bonus paid to each executive is therefore 6.66 per cent of basic salary.

Example 2
Executive cash incentives calculated by the direct method

This method employs a scale which attempts to relate the level of achievement to a bonus which is calculated as a percentage of salary. The maximum bonus paid in this example would be 20 per cent of salary.

Target to be achieved				**Bonus paid**	
90% (or below) of target profit contribution				No bonus	
91– 95%	,,	,,	,,	5 %	of salary
96–100%	,,	,,	,,	$7\frac{1}{2}$%	,, ,,
101–105%	,,	,,	,,	10 %	,, ,,
106–110%	,,	,,	,,	$12\frac{1}{2}$%	,, ,,
111–115%	,,	,,	,,	15 %	,, ,,
Above 115%	,,	,,	,,	20 %	,, ,,

In both the bonus fund and the direct methods of calculating bonus some care will be needed in specifying correctly the targets which executives can achieve. In this way a tangible and measurable contribution can be made to corporate performance. This may not be easy and will require sound and thorough analysis of executive contributions and their link to profitability. In particular, this will require the necessary detail to be included in the management accounts and the acceptance of these accounts as a measure of manager performance. Finally, the scheme should be reviewed and if necessary redesigned every three years to maintain the incentive effect. Executive incentive schemes can easily become regarded as a normal and expected part of the remuneration package.

The need for caution?

Many firms steer clear of incentive payments for management, while others have introduced them to substantially improve the remuneration and standard of living of their executives. But what is wrong with established executive remuneration to make an incentive necessary? And are the company's operations suitable for an incentive scheme to exert a significant influence on corporate performance? These questions need careful attention and accurate answers before executive incentive schemes are adopted. It could be argued that executive salaries and benefits should be enough to ensure a contribution from an employee group who are supposed to be 'concerned' about corporate well-being anyway. In any event, somebody in the company should possess the knowledge and skill to measure performance, monitor results, relate performance to pay and have the authority to make the scheme a success in the long term.

In the last analysis we may conclude that executive incentives reflect the changed attitudes among these people. They no longer identify closely with the company and have become alienated from the aims of the organizations they serve. Money cannot cure this deep-rooted problem in British industry, rather it is capable of solution by attention to organization, managerial tasks and the effectiveness of the chief executive. For the moment incentives for management at senior and middle levels may represent no more than additional complications for executive salary structures to duplicate those created among the structures for the employee groups they manage. If incentives have a place in the remuneration of executives it lies a long way behind attention to several qualitative issues affecting the performance of British managers.

Conclusion

The incentive scheme is clearly here to stay but still needs improvement. We have seen the areas where such improvements are needed, and have considered some genuine solutions, particularly for shop floor schemes. But such solutions are not always easy or simple and require considerable attention and commitment from management. Additionally there is a need to consider incentives at all levels of the organization as the elements of a performance orientated remunerations structure. The design of such incentives will require technical excellence in their design and social excellence in recognizing the presence of and allowing for the influence of behavioural factors in motivation.

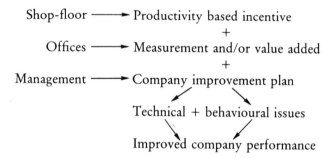

References

1 SMITH I G, 'Why wage systems fail' *Management Today.* July 1976 pp 44–106.

2 BROWN W, *Piecework abandoned.* Heinemann. 1963.

3 WALLUM P, 'Financial incentives for top executives', *Personnel Management*, Vol. 15, No. 4, April 1983 pp 32–35.

4 WALLUM P, *and* VERNON-HARCOURT T. *Monks guide to senior management incentives*, Monks Publications. 1983.

5 MALI P, *Improving total productivity*, John Wiley and Sons. 1978.

6 *Ibid* See particularly chapter 8.

7 Based on and adapted from examples provided by Wallum P *loc cit.*

Part IV

FRINGE BENEFITS

9
Benefits in remuneration

In addition to the provision of remuneration in the form of wages and salaries, the employer provides remuneration in kind which takes the form of what is often called fringe benefits. There is no common agreement on just what is included under this heading, but normally they are offered over and above the wages and salaries, as a means of improving employee well-being. In addition to the term 'fringe benefits', terms such as wages extras, perks, non-wage benefits or labour costs, hidden payroll and supplementary wage practices are used to describe these provisions. In rather typical fashion, the United States Bureau of Labour Statistics dispenses with 'fringe' and 'benefit' and adopts the mouthful, 'selected supplementary remuneration practices'. This wording emphasizes the remunerative aspect of providing benefits. It removes any hint of fringe costs which seems appropriate given that 30 to 40 per cent of pay-roll costs is hardly a fringe element, and takes out the word benefit which has a welfare connotation to it. The growth of benefits since the 1950s has resulted from two pressures: the influence of legislation and the need to offer something more than wage or salary in order to remain competitive in the labour market and offset the effects of taxation on earnings. Benefits have become an important element of remuneration, and because of their link with status, can be a cause of employee discontent. The motivational influence of benefits is too problematic to allow any definitive assessment, but their importance in the remuneration package is considerable and some attention to the subject will allow for an appreciation of benefits within a remuneration policy.

Formulating a policy

Some benefits, such as redundancy provisions and maternity leave, are required by law. Benefits, such as pensions, may be provided for moral reasons and to attract effective staff. A company car may be offered because of its value to the employee and because it makes up for taxation on earnings. Holidays may be given in the interests of employee well-being and performance and to help ensure employee goodwill. House purchase assistance, company cars and car allowances and private medical insurance may be limited to certain groups of employees where value to the company and employee status, both justify and require these perks. Benefits may be given or enhanced because other companies in the labour market provide them, or because employees demand them normally through negotiations, or because employees wish to anticipate developments. In short, benefits are provided for a multiplicity of reasons.

One overall policy for benefits may be difficult to formulate, but in this context it is useful to categorize benefits in the following way:

Security: Pensions, sick pay, redundancy cover, group life insurance and service contracts

Goodwill: Holidays, sick leave, maternity leave, compassionate leave, early retirement provisions, loan schemes, relocation assistance, house purchase assistance, car and mileage allowances, provision of car parks, provision of medical services, working clothes, provision of laundering facilities, free or subsidized transport to work, subsidized meals, company shop with discounted goods and long service awards

Performance: Company cars, medical insurance, and year end bonuses in kind which are tangible additions to the employee's standard of living.

Not all organizations provide the above benefits. During the seventies, rumours abounded about firms which provided cars for every level of management from foremen up, sent executives and their families to exotic holiday spots in the sun, and provided senior executives with luxury flats in London with some peculiar attendant benefits. This is exaggeration. The majority of companies are very careful in benefit provision and are by no means as generous as the glossy image presented in the media would sometimes suggest.

Most benefits are found under the goodwill heading. Furthermore it could be argued that the performance benefits can be categorized as goodwill or security. But this performance group is based on the importance of the benefit to the recipient, and the practice in many firms of linking their provision to the demonstrated ability as well as status of the employee. It is the case, however, that any motivation connected with these benefits will be limited to the management and directors, who are the only groups to normally receive them.

In a broader sense, all benefits help to provide a background of security and goodwill which, while not immediately motivating, can determine a climate in which a performance orientated strategy for wages and salaries is made viable. This 'enabling' aspect of benefits is often ignored or discounted by management. Yet it provides the basic security and general well-being among the work-force that leaves them free to concentrate on other elements of working life, including some fulfilment through achievement. Behavioural issues might therefore be considered in the use of benefits, with security and goodwill underpinning a positive attitude to work and the employer and providing an opportunity for higher order needs, such as self-actualization, to become motivators. Thus, employee performance is not entirely divorced from the subject of benefits.

There is some justification for arguing that management decisions concerning all benefits should be made with some consideration of the impact on wage and salary policies and the implications for performance issues. This longer term approach is certainly to be preferred to the short sighted decisions on benefits made in the sixties and seventies, which were over hasty reactions to the effects of taxation on earnings or competition in the labour market. Seen as a means of clearing away some of the obstacles to a performance orientated remuneration policy, benefits may be recognized as having some significance for organizational well-being. Below is a review of some of the major types of employee benefits.

Pension schemes

Usually considered as the most significant of benefits, and sometimes the most costly supplement to the pay-roll, pensions can be classed as deferred income. The financing of that income is normally through employee and employer contributions, although the ratio of the two contributions varies considerably, with some public and private sector employers offering non-contributory pensions to attract high calibre material into senior executive ranks. There is no doubt that pension schemes do attract employees in white-collar and managerial categories, and do generate goodwill. Their effect on blue-collar groups has been less noticeable, although there is little empirical data to prove definitively that such employees are more concerned with current income than longer term security.

Pension provisions have become complex and demand some depth of knowledge and experience from those in charge of the relevant administration. Legal and taxation issues must be considered. Approval of schemes must be obtained from the Inland Revenue, and some astute judgement is necessary if the funding of the scheme is to be balanced with maximum benefits. External advice from consultants may therefore be necessary in the early stages of introduction. Such expert advice may become all the more necessary with trade union involvement in the design and administration of the scheme, something which has increased in frequency since the 1975 Social Security Pensions Act.

The 1975 Act considerably altered pension provision in Britain, together with a new earnings related state pension scheme introduced in April 1978. This will provide a pension worth 1.25 per cent of earnings for each of the best 20 years in employment. The earnings are revalued in line with the movement of average earnings. Company pension schemes can contract out of the state scheme with a consequent reduction in National Insurance contributions. The 1975 Act also requires company pension schemes to provide the same terms to men and women. Maximum statutory provisions for pension schemes since April 1980 are as follows.

The normal retirement pension provides two thirds of the wage or salary paid in the 12 month period up to retirement with no upper limit on the amount of pay. Eligibility is 10 years service.

The lump sum option allows for 3.75 per cent of final pay to be provided at pensionable age for each year, up to a maximum of 40 years service. The ceiling figure is one and a half times final pay in cases where length of service exceeds 20 years. This provision is very popular with white-collar and management groups.

Widow's benefit is two thirds of the employee's pension which would have been achieved on retirement and a lump sum equivalent to four times his current earnings.

Widow's pension covers death in retirement and can be two thirds of the husband's pension.

The adjustment of benefit to keep pace with inflation is allowed by the Inland Revenue who will provide a figure which they consider reasonable and acceptable.

There are several formulae for determining the amount of pension. The most common determinant is final earnings in employment, and the pension may be some proportion of the wage or salary or an average of wage or salary in final years. The figure is normally multiplied by length of service or at least pensionable service. If some proportion is used this will normally be in sixtieths up to the statutory maximum of $\frac{2}{3}$ or 40/60ths.

Age of entry is clearly of crucial significance in determining the amount of benefit for the employee, and management need to ensure that the scheme provides two-thirds of income after 40 years service, and allows for late entry for those employee groups considered mobile but necessary to company operations (this will be expensive particularly for executives). Also the level of earnings on which pension is based needs careful consideration in particular for white-collar and management. The choice will be between final years earnings, or average of last five, or average of the best three out of the last 10 years service.

Early retirement pensions

This provision has always enjoyed limited popularity from the employer's point of view, but in the current recession has become a means for de-manning and reducing overheads if the resultant vacancy is not filled. The benefit is normally calculated at a rate lower than that for normal retirement in order to contain costs to the company. Until recent years, any cases of long-term disability of ill-health were treated more sympathetically, with the provision of full pension earned up to the date of early retirement or the full pension for the years between early retirement age and normal retirement age. Now companies are looking closely at the possibility of providing this same pension for early retirement above the age of 60, where this is required in the interests of reducing overheads. The cost of such provision often proves too high however, and early retirement has not yet become as popular as is generally believed.

Transfers between schemes

The older an employee becomes, the more he feels trapped by the pension rights he is afraid to lose. Thus people stay in jobs which they have long ago outgrown and where they are no longer effective to the detriment of their own and company performance. Changing jobs involves an unacceptable cost in terms of pension. There is a real need for organizations to introduce flexibility in connection with the transference of pension rights particularly for employees who need wide experience and where career progression is best gained in more than one company. Even where such transferability is possible, however, the transfer value is usually such that the pension scheme in the organization to which an employee moves, provides a pension which is worth less than the accrued pension rights with the previous employer. The only solution to this problem is some form of 'topping up' arrangement with additional contributions from the employee.

In the case of senior executives and directors, separate and additional pension schemes can be established under the terms of the 1973 Finance Act (sometimes termed 'top hat' arrangements). The National Association of Pension Funds reported in 1979 that 47 per cent of companies provided such arrangements for senior management and directors, with 37 per cent using a topping up scheme to make up any losses caused by these employees changing jobs.

Financing pension schemes

The ceiling on employee contributions is 15 per cent of wage or salary. The 1979 NAPF survey revealed that 81 per cent of schemes were contributory and the remaining 19 per cent non-contributory. Tax relief is forthcoming to employees in contributory schemes plus a refund after a short period of membership. Joint interest by employer and employee is normally claimed to be a major benefit of contributory schemes, but there is no doubt that with the non-contributory type of scheme, a very attractive benefit is offered to employees with lower administrative costs for the employer. The overall cost of non-contributory schemes can be higher, but even this can be offset if earnings levels are lowered to reflect the size of the financial advantage to the employee derived from the scheme.

Funding arrangements for contributions (employer and employee) are usually through investments in insurance policies, securities, shares and even valuable objects such as paintings. Strangely very few schemes are insured, 23 per cent according to the 1979 NAPF survey.

Information of pension arrangements and practice can be obtained from the National Association of Pension Funds, the Occupational Pensions Board and Incomes Data Services.

Concluding note

The achilles heel of these schemes is that they reward length of service at the expense of employee development and career progression. This has become a serious depressant of employee motivation and performance and requires urgent change.

Company cars

This is a key part of the remuneration package for senior executives, sales staff and directors. During the seventies it also became increasingly important to some middle managers. In 1979 the Inland Revenue estimated that cars accounted for 80 per cent of the total 'cake' of fringe benefits excluding pensions. Cars are an emotive issue, and this writer has at times concluded that the company car causes more frustration discussion and enthusiasm than any other element of remuneration. Many managers have declined or accepted posts purely on the basis of the provision of an automobile. The car provided is usually of a higher specification than the manager would purchase privately, and it often appears that the car is out of line with the employee's general standard of living.

The 1982 Annual Survey of Executive Salaries and Fringe Benefits prepared by Inbucon[1] found that 78 per cent of managers surveyed had a company car, and in the case of those earning over £10,000 the figure rises to 85 per cent. The 1982 British Institute of Management survey report No 53 by M Woodmansey[2] claimed that 70 per cent of managers probably have a company car, and found 47 per cent of those surveyed regarded the car as essential in a new job offer and 29 per cent regarded it as fairly important.

The 1976 Finance Act brought the company car under the scrutiny of the Inland Revenue, and companies should regularly monitor the tax regulations for cars. The benefit is taxable for individuals earning more than £8,500 per annum (a figure which has been static since 1979 and since then has resulted in a doubling of the number of employees liable for tax on company cars). Free petrol for drivers of company cars which are used for private as well as business use is also taxable, and in April 1983 new tax scales will be introduced. This change means that free petrol will be taxed irrespective of how it is provided and will close certain loopholes. The 1983 scales are provided below.

Table 9
Tax scales on company cars from April 6th, 1983

Cost of car	Engine capacity	Tax Liability	
		Car under 4yrs old	Car over 4yrs old
Up to £14,000	Up to 1300 cc	£325	£225
	1301cc to 1800cc	£425	£300
	Over 1800cc	£650	£450
£14,000–£21,000		£950	£650
Over £21,000		£1,500	£1,000

Despite such tax changes, company cars are likely to remain very popular benefits, but the cost to the employer can be considerable, and the company car policy is usually determined at board level. Car allocation for sales and service personnel is usually straightforward, but needs careful handling for executives. Only at senior levels will status be a significant issue in car allocation. For other levels the need for travel should be the major determinant, although this is not always the case, and the company Granada or Cortina or Cavalier or Ambassador may spend most of its life in the car park (despite the fact that the lower the business mileage the greater the tax liability).

Table 10
Tax scales on petrol from April 6, 1983

Cylinder capacity	Cash equivalent
Up to 1300cc	£325
1300cc to 1800cc	£425
Over 1800cc	£650

The motor industry in Britain relies heavily on the sale of fleet cars. A browse through a Ford brochure, for example, provides a classic case of a range of cars tailor-made to the rungs of the executive ladder. The top of the range, Granada Ghia with all the extras is for the chairman of the Board: lesser Granadas for the directors. The better equipped Cortinas (or now the Sierra) for senior managers, and the lesser Sierra brethren for middle managers and sales staff. A car for junior management, if thought necessary, could be taken from the ranks of Escort and Fiesta models. It is normal for companies to buy British, although some imports are gaining more than a toe-hold, particularly at the top of the executive ladder.

Factors to be considered in buying a car or range of cars include the need to represent the individual's status and the desired image for the company. Business requirements must be met, but there may be a case for balancing this with the personal preference of the company car driver. Maintenance costs and reliability must be at acceptable levels and the car should have an acceptable residual value when it comes to be sold on the second-hand market.

At senior executive levels some choice among comparable models is normally offered, with choice more restricted further down the organization. Basic specification and any optional extras such as a stereo radio-cassette or alloy wheels will need to be determined within the 'budget' allocated to the car purchase. This will have to be calculated together with insurance and running costs and the replacement policy. The amount of company financed private mileage will also need to be decided. The initial cost of the car will be substantially lower than the list price because of the fleet discount, although the size of discount can vary among manufacturers and indeed among different models from the same manufacturer. In the current economic climate companies are looking for cars with a lower initial purchase price. They are moving to smaller engines and less in the way of equipment or moving to smaller cars altogether but with a rather more luxurious specification. Replacement normally takes place between two and three years from purchase and with 40,000 to 60,000 miles on the clock, depending on the assessment of future running costs against current resale value.

The British Institute of Management report mentioned above calculates the value of a car as a £1,000 to £2,000 addition to gross salary, depending on the model of car considered. Depreciation alone on a £5,500 family saloon could be £1,375 in the first year of ownership, with £500 to £600 for petrol (assuming 10,000 miles at 30 mpg), over £100 for insurance and about £80 for servicing. Added together, this exceeds £2000, and tax would have to be incorporated into this figure to provide equivalent gross earnings. On larger and more luxurious cars such as Ford Granadas, Rovers and Vauxhall Royales, the addition to gross salary is considerably more.

Termination of employment usually means withdrawal of the car, if the reason is incompetence. With redundancy, cars are normally included in the terms for severence with employees being given the option to buy the car at a price lower than the market rate. In these circumstances, it is useful to deduct the value of the car from any figure offered as compensation. Where the employee is moved to a position which is not eligible for a company car, the new salary should represent a sufficient increase to cover the cost of private car purchase. If the salary cannot be so improved, the individual concerned can be offered the car at a favourable price and with the offer of interest free or low interest financing arrangements.

Concluding note

That the company car is a means of improving manager performance remains unproven. The glossy view of the executive being spurred on up the company ladder not just by salary and status but by the prospect of a more attractive car does not seem to hold true in the real world of corporate life. It is also interesting to note that company cars are more popular in Britain than in most other industrial nations. Indeed this writer worked in Canadian and American companies where the only company car was a chauffeur-driven Cadillac for the chairman.

The provision of company cars can cause problems. It has far too much unnecessary influence in individual career decisions, causes resentment among those without cars, and is an administrative and cost burden for the company. To what extent a car makes up for low executive salaries is difficult to determine, but certainly they are used to balance out the effects of taxation. Whatever the original reasons for providing company cars, they have become an expected part of the executive's remuneration package at a time when executive salary structures often remain devoid of effective design and rationality. A useful alternative to the company car is the interest free loan for the purposes of car purchase where a car is necessary for occasional business use. It might be reasonable to ask, however, just how many companies are convinced that the whole fleet is being optimally utilized in the interests of the company's well-being.

Car and mileage allowance

In addition to interest free car loans, an annual car allowance or mileage allowance is a viable alternative to the company car. The car allowance can help the individual obtain and maintain a car in keeping with his status and occasional business usage. Mileage allowances are paid for actual journeys made in the employee's own car on company business. Such allowances vary. At December 1982 a spot survey of eleven organizations revealed a low of 18 pence per mile and a high of 28 pence per mile, with the majority clustered in the 18 pence to 22 pence range.

Sick pay

A scheme for sick pay provision is now normal in employing organizations, and many improvements have been made in this area over the past two decades. Thus sick pay schemes are able to offer some degree of financial security to employees. Some extension of cover is often made by companies' on compassionate grounds to help the terminally ill, or the seriously ill when a return to work is delayed.

As these words are written, changes in sick pay provision are taking place as a result of the Social Security and Housing Benefits Bill which became law on June 28th, 1982 and which took effect from April 1983. All employees paying full National Insurance contributions are covered, new statutory duties are placed on the employer and the unions have reacted to the new legislation as a threat to the sick pay entitlements they have already negotiated.

Employers will be required to pay statutory sick pay to employees for the first eight weeks of calculated sick pay and then reclaim the money from the government: the payments will be deductable from employer National Insurance contributions. Records will have to be maintained for inspection by National Insurance officials, and employers will have to pay the National Insurance contributions on the statutory sick pay. The period for which ssp is provided is eight weeks, after which the employee receives State Sickness Benefit. Figure 21 on page 208 provides an in-company procedure for dealing with ssp.

A major cause of trade union concern about the new legislation is that the level of benefit will be less than the current entitlement for the vast majority of employees. This is because ssp will be liable to tax and NI contributions and will be paid at a flat rate with no additions for dependents. Some unions have responded to this development with attempts to renegotiate existing sick pay provision to maintain benefit after the new legislation takes effect.

One of the first companies to amend sick pay arrangements from April 1983 was the Westland Group whose scheme was reviewed by Incomes Data Services in issue Number 8, October 1982. The main features of this scheme are as follows.

The employee receives full salary when sick (sick pay = income – ssp or income – any other benefit).

Statutory Sick Pay is provided in addition to the above on condition that the employee complies with government regulations to qualify for ssp.

When sickness benefit is exhausted the employee must go through a new qualification period dependent on his or her length of service in the tax year in which the illness started.

The minimum length of service for entitlement is eight weeks and the levels of provision are as follows:

less than 12 months service—8 weeks in tax year.
more than 1 year less than 3 years—12 weeks in tax year.
more than 3 years less than 5 years—20 weeks in tax year.
more than 5 years less than 10 years—32 weeks in tax year.
over 10 years service—51* weeks in tax year.

* includes holiday entitlement in the year in which sickness absence occurs.

1983 will doubtless see the introduction of many similar arrangements which represent an improvement on what was available before, particularly in the areas of length of service and entitlement. For further

Figure 21
In-company procedure for Statutory Sick Pay after April 1983

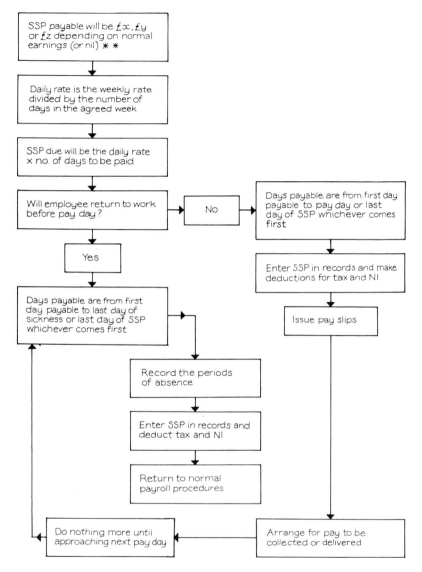

SSP payable will be £x, £y or £z depending on normal earnings (or nil) ✳ ✳

Daily rate is the weekly rate divided by the number of days in the agreed week

SSP due will be the daily rate × no. of days to be paid

Will employee return to work before pay day?

No

Days payable are from first day payable to pay day or last day of SSP whichever comes first

Yes

Enter SSP in records and make deductions for tax and NI

Days payable are from first day payable to last day of sickness or last day of SSP whichever comes first

Issue pay slips

Record the periods of absence

Enter SSP in records and deduct tax and NI

Return to normal payroll procedures

Do nothing more until approaching next pay day

Arrange for pay to be collected or delivered

✳✳ Where earnings are below £32.50 pw no SSP is payable; for earnings between £32.50 and £48.49pw, £27.20 is payable. For earnings between £48.50 and £64.99 pw, £33.75 is payable; for earnings over £65 pw, £40.25 is payable. These figures are subject to review every autumn and subject to change in the following April.

information on the government legislation the reader is referred to the 'Employers Guide to ssp' published by the Department of Health and Social Security.

Medical insurance

The provision of medical insurance has traditionally been limited to directors and senior executives in order to ensure that medical treatment is obtained at a time which is convenient to the company. Lengthening waiting lists for treatment under the National Health Service has recently given rise to some employee demand for private health cover particularly among white-collar staffs, and some companies have thus adopted a company financed scheme or group scheme in which employees can participate at a discount on the normal premium. At the least, the provision of private medical insurance is a means of ensuring minimum dislocation to the work of key employees, and can also be a means of generating goodwill among employees.

Holidays

The taking of a holiday from work as a means to maintaining the effectiveness of employees has long been practised in Britain, and indeed gave rise to the British seaside resort. In recent years, holiday provision has been increasing. Perhaps the most significant development was the 1979 National Engineering Agreement, which increased the annual entitlement for 1½ million workers from 23 days in 1979 to 25 days in November 1982. Five weeks entitlement has become an objective for most trade unions representing manual workers, and by 1984 a large number of companies will see the attainment of this goal. There has also been an increasing tendency for manual workers to receive service related holidays rising from 36 per cent of the manual work-force in 1978 to 40 per cent in 1980 (Department of Employment Gazette, April 1981).

These improvements for manual workers have placed pressure on white-collar unions to seek additional holiday entitlements to maintain the differential between their members and manual groups. Normally, such entitlements are linked to service, with the current aim for some unions being a minimum of 25 days leave for up to five years service and a maximum of 32 days leave for 25 years and over.

In October 1981, Incomes Data Services Ltd reported the following range of entitlements in 84 private and public sector organizations:

Number of days holiday	Number of organizations
Less than 20	7
20	24
21	2
22	12
23	10
24	6
25	11
Over 25	12

Source: Incomes Data Services Ltd, Report 25, 1 October 1981, p 3.

The lowest holiday entitlement revealed was 15 days in the retail trade and the highest was 30 days in the clothing and textile industry. The same Incomes Data Services report found the following provisions for holiday pay. In 30 organizations, white-collar staff were paid as follows: 14 firms provided normal salary, 11 provided basic pay, four provided basic pay plus regular allowances and one paid average earnings.

In 21 firms manual workers were paid as follows: workers received average earnings in 11, basic pay plus allowances was paid in nine firms, and basic pay was provided by one firm.

16 companies did not distinguish between white-collar and manual groups, and in this case six paid basic pay plus allowances, four paid average earnings, four provided basic pay and two paid normal earnings to all employees.

One increasing problem in connection with holiday entitlement is the request for extended leave, particularly to visit relatives outside Europe. There are several ways of dealing with this issue. Some companies allow employees to take all their annual leave at once, others allow employees to carry their leave entitlement forward into the next year, and some firms allow extended leave on the basis of discretionary approval by management. Formal policies on extended leave are also increasing and IDS Study 251 provides useful examples of these.

Some employees have responsibilities which limit the opportunity to take the full holiday entitlement. Middle and senior management are vulnerable to this problem, as are supervisory staff in certain process technologies, maintenance workers and those responsible for computer systems which operate 24 hours a day and seven days every week. A minimum annual leave is often stipulated to deal with this problem, or payment can be made in lieu of the holiday entitlement or the unused leave can be accrued into later years.

Clearly holidays have become an important fringe benefit with ever increasing generosity in the level of provision. But management should beware of being too generous. The current recession has made it convenient to agree increased holiday entitlements, but this could backfire in better times when output is the main requirement. Recent improvements may have been awarded without any reference to the longer term implications, particularly in terms of production and costs.

Compassionate leave

Employee requests for compassionate leave are usually made in connection with some emotional crisis, and should therefore receive fair and speedy consideration. Such leave will normally be given for the following reasons:

   (i)   death of close relative and funeral
  (ii)   serious illness of close relative
 (iii)   marriage
  (iv)   hospital, dental and other personal appointments
   (v)   jury service
  (vi)   day release for studies
 (vii)   training leave for Territorial Army service
(viii)   religious holidays for ethnic minority employees
  (ix)   time off in lieu of overtime
   (x)   civic duties incurred by an employee (eg council work).

Maternity leave

The basic provisions for maternity leave are covered by the 1975 Employment Protection Act and are not generous. Some organizations have therefore found it worthwhile to improve on the statutory entitlement. These improvements can be achieved by allowing longer periods of leave and retention of job entitlement after the birth, and/or by reducing the minimum length of service requirement for maternity leave from 24 months to 12 months.

For white-collar staff some companies provide up to six weeks paternity leave. But this provision is still quite rare and many companies prefer to allow the father to attend to his family duties through the *ad hoc* provision of compassionate leave or the taking of normal holiday entitlement.

Financial assistance

These provisions are scarce and tend to be limited to white-collar and management groups within the financial sector organizations such as banking and insurance. Loans for annual season tickets in London and the main conurbations have become popular for white-collar staff. In the case of senior executives, financial assistance with house purchase is sometimes provided. This may take the form of an interest free bridging loan to speed up the move to the new house, or in a few very rare cases, a company mortgage.

There is no doubt that the provision of low interest loans in the financial sector is able to offer a considerable incentive to loyalty and contribution among employees. For the vast majority of companies however, it is impossible to tie up financial resources in this way.

Assistance with moving expenses is often provided to newly recruited white-collar staff and those who move at company request. Payments may cover fees to estate agents and solicitors, and the costs of removal and storage. In some cases, instead of reimbursing specific outlays the payment may take the form of an overall disturbance allowance calculated as a percentage of the salary. Ten per cent is a normal amount and it is usually free of tax.

Other forms of financial assistance to employees include the reimbursement of course and examination fees for training which is work related, discounts on company products and on products sold in a company shop. In the case of senior white-collar and management staffs, the employer may pay for subscriptions to job related professional associations, and with senior executives provide credit cards for business expenses.

Choosing to provide such financial assistance requires a careful consideration of the costs involved and of the opportunities for abuse of the provisions together with a full regard for the tax implications. Against these considerations the advantages deriving from these benefits, particularly in terms of employee goodwill, can be evaluated.

Discounts on company products and services

Some people are fortunate enough to work for companies manufacturing products or providing services which are in regular demand by the public and therefore employees. Domestic consumer durables, confectionery and grocery items, clothing and transport are good examples. Many companies offer substantial discounts to employees, as much as 25 to 30 per cent on the products they make or sell. As with the company car such provisions represent a substantial and tangible addition to income and are an effective 'tax dodge'. When an employee can obtain televisions, refrigerators, cookers, suits and dresses, food and transport substantially below the going rate he is left with a significant amount of

Table 11
Redundancy and severance awards 1981

Organisation	Payment
Dunlop (Scheme A)	Age 18–40 RPA+40%+4 weeks' pay ⎱ Age 41–49 RPA+40%+4 weeks' pay ⎰ £130 limit Age 50–65 RPA+65%+8 weeks' pay not applied
(Scheme B)	RPA+½ week's pay per year of service up to 20 yrs RPA+1½ weeks' pay per year of service over 20 yrs £130 limit applied to RPA but not additional payment. With 20 or more years' service, four extra weeks' pay.
Esso	Up to age 39 1½ weeks' pay per year of service 40–49 1½ weeks' pay per 6 mths' service + three weeks' pay for each 6 months' service after age 40, max. of 104 weeks' pay.
Ford	Up to age 41 one week's pay per year of service 41–65 (or 60) 1½ weeks' pay per year of service No upper limit on service, payment is made for years of service below age 18.
Gas Supply	18–21 One week per year of service max 20 years 22–40 1½ weeks per year of service max 20 years 41–64 two weeks per year of service max 20 years Employees aged 50 or over with 10 or more years' service are entitled to an additional 33⅓%. Employees with two years' service since age 18 are entitled to an additional 25%.
International Harvester (basic)	Up to age 21 two weeks' pay per year of service 22–40 2½ weeks' pay per year of service 41–64(59) three weeks' pay per year of service.
Metal Box	three weeks' pay per year of service plus ½ week's pay for those years when employee aged 40 or more.
Pirelli	two–20 years RPA+50% 20 years or more RPA+100%.
Pilkington	Age 18–29 1.75 × RPA Age 30–39 2.00 × RPA Age 40–49 2.50 × RPA Age 50–54 3.25 × RPA Age 55 2.82 × RPA Age 56 2.55 × RPA Age 57 2.29 × RPA Age 58 2.03 × RPA Age 59 1.77 × RPA Age 60–64 1.50 × RPA

Source: Incomes Data Services Ltd. Study 250, September 1981, p 5.

income to spend on other aspects of life. A company shop is often provided to deal with this service, and can take up some considerable administrative resources in the larger firms. Discounts often make up for salaries which are less than competitive, but nonetheless may be seen to provide an unfair advantage to some groups of workers.

Redundancy

Some of the benefits discussed in this chapter are not so much elements of remuneration as of compensation. This is certainly the case with redundancy provisions. Furthermore despite the publicity given to some redundancy payments, particularly in the steel industry, payments to the newly unemployed often stay close to the minimum specified by the Employment Protection Act (Consolidation) 1978. Admittedly more profitable organizations have seen the negotiation of improved redundancy terms. But in the present recession, it is difficult to see how some redundancy payments help to maintain some vestige of the employee's standard of living for the lengthy period it can now take to find new employment.

Redundancy payments are made up of two components, statutory payment and company top up. The Incomes Data Services Ltd Study 250 of September 1981 found that company top ups of statutory provisions vary widely, although the amounts of redundancy payments have generally increased over the last few years. The top up can take the form of statutory payment plus one or more payments under separate headings or enhanced statutory provision, which can also include additional payments such as a service related lump-sum or payment in lieu of notice. Table 11 on page 213 provides some details of redundancy and severance awards for some of the companies covered in the IDS Study 250.

Harmonization of benefits

This refers to the process of bringing manual and white-collar conditions of service and work practices into some kind of alignment. Harmonization is in fact one of three ways of achieving such alignment and is normally concerned with particular conditions of service. Single Status for all employees covers all conditions and work practices, while Staff Status refers to the conferring of staff conditions on certain manual groups such as skilled workers.

There is no clear evidence on which of these three approaches to eroding differentials is the most favoured. The aims are normally the

214

improvement of labour productivity, simplification of pay-roll procedures, improvements in employee attitudes and improvements in the recruitment and retention of manpower.

Conditions which have been subjected to harmonization include time (changes in hours worked, elimination of clocking arrangements and deductions for lateness), leave (improvements in provision), sick pay and pensions (changes in eligibility, contributions and benefits), security of employment (guaranteed working week and redundancy provisions) and changes in other fringe benefits and catering facilities. In practically all cases these changes have been aimed at the harmonization of manual conditions with white-collar conditions.

Conclusions

The need for fringe benefits to allow for (if not actually promote) employee mobility is long overdue. The acquisition of wide ranging experience, and a willingness to move, are not encouraged by current benefit policies. Dealing with this problem is now a major challenge to companies desirous of obtaining the brain-power and commitment necessary to see them through to the 21st century.

On a less polemic note, fringe benefits are mainly of importance to a strategy for remuneration in the way they provide goodwill and security. Against this background or climate, management have the opportunity to implement a performance orientated remuneration policy. Benefits now represent a considerable proportion of pay-roll costs, and many benefits are regarded as necessary elements of the terms of employment. Investment at this level in the provision of some degree of financial security, and perquisites has some motivational effect even if it is indirect and long-term. Therefore, the formulation of a policy for benefits may require an examination of longer run implications for employee and company performance, rather than just a loosely planned and short-term reaction to employee demands and minimum legal requirements. The value of any benefit to the employee and the resultant goodwill also require evaluation against cost to the employer. This evaluation exercise may prove the old claim that investment in employee performance can involve more than just take-home pay.

References

1 *The 1982 annual survey of executive salaries and fringe benefits.* Inbucon 1982.

2 WOODMONSEY M, *BIM survey report No 53.* British Institute of Management 1982.

Part V

CONCLUSION

10
Retrospect and prospect

The underlying assumptions behind the management of remuneration as presented in this book are that organizations have purposes, are peopled by individuals who have needs (social and material or economic) and that these two elements of purpose and need should be linked. A link has been suggested in the form of a strategic performance orientated perspective of remuneration. This should give purpose to management decisions about pay and benefits in the areas of design of structures, the levels and elements of pay within the structures, and the provision of incentives and fringe benefits. Within this process of decision making, management should pay attention to behavioural and economic influences on pay determination and a review of this managerial task now follows.

Structure and process in the management of remuneration

Pay systems are more often than not characterized by rules and procedures. Job evaluation schemes, incentive schemes, the provision of overtime, allowances and fringe benefits require such rules and procedures to allow for common agreement and understanding among management and employees. Despite the presence of this 'structured' element of remuneration, we have seen that order and rationality can break down and remuneration systems, which once gave every indication of being based on principles and rationality, begin to move out of management's understanding and control. No matter how effectively the structure of remuneration is managed, we need to remember that structure of itself does nothing.

The distortion of structural elements is brought about by the indeterminate economic and social dynamics of relative power, influence and control within collective bargaining and in the labour market. It is also affected by inter-personal relationships, individual

219

needs, motivation, and perceptions of equity. These dynamic elements make up the *process* which influences the outcome of management decisions about the *structure* of remuneration. Process refers to the actual conditions which influence performance. Structure refers to the hopes or intentions determined under the heading of performance and is a function of the regulations which management think are appropriate. When drawing up the regulations, attention is given to the needs of the organization first and the needs of individuals second.

Because employees' needs come second, management run the risk of designing remuneration with little consideration of the process system which can actually make remuneration work to specification. The process elements are the fuel which can drive the structure as management wish, or destroy it. If remuneration structures are not to be destroyed, management should recognize the need for congruence between the management of structure and the management of process: in chapter 2 it was revealed that this requires attention to the economic forces in the organizations' external environment and the behavioural issues in the internal environment.

It must be admitted that achieving some degree of balance between structure and process is difficult, and the problem underlines the argument that there is no simple solution or technique for the task of effectively managing remuneration. Therefore, a greater awareness and understanding of the wide-ranging and complex issues affecting remuneration (and its contribution to organization well-being) is the prerequisite to the successful application of methods and techniques presented in this book. With such an understanding, there is more likelihood of realizing the following requirements.

Requirements for the effective management of remuneration

In the first instance we may consider understanding and responding to the following recent developments or pressures:

   (i)   the need to offset the costs of inflation through the better use of all production resources

  (ii)   the need to survive in conditions of recession through the reduction of costs and the better use of resources

 (iii)   the need to recognize and cope with new attitudes to work and managerial authority

 (iv)   the need to reassess managerial responsibilities for remuneration and return such responsibility to line managers

(v)   the need to restimulate the incentive culture in tune with corporate requirements

(vi) the need to restore equity in remuneration structures which have seen differentials distorted by uncontrolled economic and social pressure in the past

(vii) the need to eliminate fragmentation and complexity in remuneration structures.

The management responses to these problems may be facilitated by attention to the following strategic elements:

(i)   the definition of objectives for remuneration which accord with the purposes of the organization

(ii) the development of a strategy which guides managerial decisions in line with remuneration objectives

(iii) managerial decisions should be based on an understanding of the process and structure elements of remuneration in the interests of achieving some control of the former in the pursuit of stability in the latter.

In turn the strategic elements will require the following detail improvement:

(i)   the co-ordination of line management decision making with personnel information and specialist knowledge

(ii) an acceptance that people are the key to corporate performance, and the replacement of lip-service to the people factor by the effective management of motivation at work

(iii) the recruitment and development of effective people

(iv) the design of remuneration structures which are consistent in their provision of reward and reflection of contribution

(v) the provision of an adequate and equitable remuneration

(vi) some attempt at the greater involvement of employees in decisions about remuneration.

A strategic framework for guidance

There must be hope that management decisions about remuneration can be improved (in terms of results) when based on a strategic approach. Furthermore, these decisions should have relevance to the needs of the organization and employees. The need for strategy derives from the direction or guidance required for management decision making and taking. That objectives are achieved may matter less than the provision of purpose and guidance for the consistent use by management of the techniques, methods and provisions discussed in sections 2, 3 and 4 of this book. We may now ask what prospect is there of this approach being realized more widely than at present, and the answer may be gleaned by the reader from reference to current and future developments in remuneration.

At the beginning of 1983, the following remuneration issues are attracting attention:

(i) the use of computers to store and update data on pay and benefits
(ii) methods for payment to employees, particularly the move away from the use of cash and the pay packet
(iii) incentive payment schemes
(iv) changes in benefit provision, particularly statutory sick pay and pensions
(v) changes to certain provisions within a process of harmonization.

The use of computers

The storage, update and retrieval of personnel information on main frame computers is by now a well established practice in many of the medium sized and large organizations. But it is still amazing to find many British firms either limiting computer applications to engineering and financial matters, or not using computer facilities at all. In the latter case, one wonders what school leavers will think of such employers after gaining 'hands on' experience with micro-computers as part of their education. It is probably the micro-computer which offers the greatest potential assistance to personnel departments, and in particular for storing and updating data for remuneration. Many companies store pay details of all kinds on 'micros' and use them to print out pay-roll data, such as incentive bonus, shift premiums, pension contribution payments and so on. Ever larger memories (the Ram) increase the data storage and handling capacity making the micro a very real alternative to the main frame computer for personnel work. The effect on the manual storage and handling of remuneration data can be considerable, with the number of staff responsible for this task often reduced by half and the processing of information speeded up. Indeed the micro makes a complex task much easier and the complexity of remuneration structures sorely begs to be handled by this very useful management aid and work-horse.

Methods of payment

Methods of payment involve a change from cash to non-cash alternatives. There are three main reasons for this:

(i) the growing belief that handling cash is dangerous and vulnerable to pay-roll robberies, and mugging of the employee on his way home
(ii) cash payment methods are expensive and inefficient
(iii) the use of cash perpetuates the blue-collar and white-collar split.

This development is also being accompanied by a move to monthly pay for all categories of employees.

The use of cash payments incurs considerable security and handling costs. The most cost effective alternative is the *automated credit transfer*, although the system requires a computer and the services of Bankers Automated Clearing Services Ltd. *Paper credit transfer* avoids the use of a computer (the employer merely giving the appropriate information and cheques to employees' banks), but is more expensive to process, incurs bank charges, and is slower than the automated transfer. *Cheques* are an even more expensive method of payment and require considerable resources in the pay-roll department. *Giro cash cheques* are expensive because of Post Office charges.

By switching from weekly to monthly payments, employers will enjoy the greatest financial benefits. Pay will be calculated less frequently, and more importantly, company cash flows should improve because payment will of course be made one month in arrears. Some companies have also switched to two payments per month, or one payment per two weeks to simplify calculations and gain some financial benefit. This provides a half-way approach where monthly payments are not acceptable to employees. Simpler calculations also characterize the payment every four weeks approach. Weekly non-cash methods are possible, but the expensive use of cheques may be necessary to ensure quick enough payment within the short time scale.

The switch from cash is of some significance for in 1979 some $13\frac{1}{2}$ million employees were paid weekly in cash: this figure included 77 per cent of all manual workers and 34 per cent of non-manual employees, 55 per cent of non-manual were on cashless methods and 11 per cent of manual.[1] The trend to cashless pay was most marked between 1970 and 1976, but the slow-down since 1976 ended with a campaign to change payment methods launched by the 12 High Street banks in winter 1981. (This was prompted by public discussion, boosted by the June 1981

Central Policy Review Staff publication on the subject.) In response to this 'Think Tank' report, the Institute of Personnel Management provided comment which sums up the present thinking on the subject: that the banks should offer more flexible hours, more cash dispensers, and better services. The Institute also voiced concern about the level of bank charges facing employees moving to non-cash payment. Should these conditions be met, the Institute was prepared to support the repeal of the Truck Acts (1831), which gives manual workers the right to be paid in coin of the realm.

There has been some question as to whether non-cash payment is specifically excluded, and one County Court judgement and the Payment of Wages Act 1960 provide for exceptions, including cheques made out to cash, credit transfers, postal orders and money orders. To switch from cash, however, employers must conform to a predetermined procedure (a written request from each employee) or incur a fine up to £200. The reader will now have realized why the move to cashless pay has been slow to date. Additionally, attitudes among management, unions and employees have been an obstacle.

Government moves on the repeal of the Truck Acts are difficult to forecast but some amendments in this decade do seem likely. With such changes, banks, managers and employees are likely to respond positively although at what rate of change is debatable.

The removal of differences in payment methods between manual and non-manual groups would help in the process of harmonization, and perhaps speed up the move from fragmented pay structure to consolidated payments. Certainly this would help in achieving the kinds of moves to simpler structures recommended elsewhere in this book, but it is remarkable perhaps that those who manage remuneration have left developments in thinking to the banks and government agencies. Again we find management responding to, rather than anticipating, events. Such anticipation may, of course, require strategy and policy as pre-requisites.

Incentive payment schemes

The current interest here is reportedly in incentive schemes for senior executives and in the improvement of work measurement and the application of techniques to work not previously covered by measurement, particularly clerical and technical operations. The hope must be that unlike the 1960s and 1970s, when the search was for a solution to a problem with pay in particular areas of work or with particular groups of workers, the search is now spurred on by an appreciation of the longer term benefits deriving from strategically developed improvements in employee motivation and performance.

Changes in benefit provision

Changes in benefit provision, particularly the 1982/83 developments affecting sick pay, may reveal an interesting change in government policy for benefits. The present administration has proved anxious to reduce government sick pay provision while at the same time causing employing organizations to review and indeed improve their own levels of provision. It is interesting to speculate how similar changes would work out in the area of pensions.

Remuneration changes through harmonization

Remuneration changes brought about by harmonization are linked to the issue of the shorter working weeek. At the centre of these developments has been the implementation (in October 1981) of the 1979 national engineering agreement which pushed the working week to below 39 hours. Some firms, particularly in the chemical and construction industries, have gone as low as $37\frac{1}{2}$ hours per week. Study 264 published by Incomes Data Services Ltd in April 1982 reveals two types of management approach to the issue as follows:[2]

(i) a tactical approach in firms struggling to survive and obtaining changes in working practices for a relatively small change in working hours or in firms trying to avoid industrial action by taking one hour off Friday to contain costs.

(ii) a strategic approach in pursuit of the objectives of greater utilization of capital and labour and/or the harmonization of hours and patterns of work.

The IDS report emphasizes that in the second approach, companies were as concerned to increase the amount of productive working time as to implement the reduction in hours. Clearly this strategic approach represents the kind of performance orientation appropriate to effective decisions on remuneration. On the issue of greater productivity, the reduction in working hours has been accompanied by agreements on the improvement of machine utilization, involving the abolition of breaks and new shift arrangements.

Harmonization deals with a problem which is unique to Britain; differences in employment conditions between manual and non-manual employees. Trade unions are currently pressing for a harmonized working week of 35 hours, although the overwhelming majority of employers are unwilling to go below 37 hours. The general feeling among employers is that a 37 hour target could be achieved by 1985 depending on the amount of any recovery in the economy.

Reductions in the working week have been paid for by adjustments to incentive schemes. Manual workers may improve output to help pay for a one hour reduction. White-collar employees working in work measurement based schemes have agreed to do 36 hours and 25 minutes work in 35 hours. In piecework schemes employees have been required to produce 40 piecework hours of work in 39.

Overtime working has also been adjusted to pay for the reduction. In the building industry, overtime premiums are provided after 40 hours and not 39.

Some firms have actually traded hours for money, and IDS Study 264 reports the arrangements at Reckitt and Colmans food and wine division. Employees were offered the following four alternatives:

(i) a percentage increase in pay with implementation of hours reduction in October 1981
(ii) a higher increase in pay with hours reduction effective in April 1982
(iii) an even higher increase in pay but no reduction in hours
(iv) a two stage pay increase with reduction in hours from January 1982.

Clearly the issue of the shorter working week has become important in developments affecting remuneration, and the resultant harmonization of hours might be accompanied by further harmonization in elements of pay and benefits. The linking of these developments to a productivity or performance strategy is to be encouraged.

The need for simpler remuneration

The goal of harmonization in particular leads attention to the need for simplification in the pay and conditions provided for various employee groups. Complex remuneration structures make the path of developing a strategy for remuneration difficult and rational controllable structures impossible to achieve. But there are now signs that companies are introducing or considering ways of simplifying pay structures to allow for consolidated payments. So far this has mainly involved limited harmonization as discussed above, reductions in overtime working and the replacement of bonuses. Thus pay is for standard hours combining basic payment and performance bonus; a basic or time or attendance rate of £90 plus a £25 bonus becomes a consolidated payment of £115 per week. Unfortunately, this encouraging trend is cancelled out by companies which persist in paying several premium rates for overtime and shift working. More worrying is the tendency to introduce new elements of pay such as attendance allowances. This fragmentation of pay is peculiar to British organizations, and is the most serious roadblock to more effective management of remuneration.

Final note

Those who have stayed the course through this work may appreciate that the various 'bits and pieces' of remuneration are difficult to combine in one package. Indeed the only means of assembling a remuneration policy which can sensibly stitch together all the elments of pay and benefits is through effective management in general and not just the effective management of remuneration on its own. Making remuneration right should be a function of making the whole organization effective.

Therefore, effective organizations and effective management are the prerequisites for effective remuneration policies, strategies, decisions and structures. Some of the failures and problems discussed in this book are a result of remuneration being managed and handled as if it were a prerequisite to effective organizations and management. But such an approach can never work, and the evidence to support this claim is found in the distorted pay structures, uncontrolled labour costs, failed incentive schemes and low levels of achievement which litter the post-war history of British industry.

Knowing where they want the company to go and the necessary improvements needed to get there allows executives to specify the requirements in all aspects of company operations. Among such 'specifications' we should find the remuneration structures, techniques and levels of provision. Therefore a theme of this book is repeated: remuneration should be contingent upon corporate policy which in turn is contingent upon the particular social and economic and other operating variables which influence strategic choices.

Effective remuneration as with any aspect of company work, is determined by the quality of senior executives and the climate of management they create. But there is no one best way of ensuring success for remuneration policies and their implementation. Executives have to persevere at finding out what works in their organization and must evolve a remuneration package to suit. If incentive schemes, job evaluation and other techniques play a minor role in that package we should not be surprised. The Japanese have not needed the incentives we use, yet they are successful; they do not use job evaluation as we do but they seem to suffer far less than Britain from friction on the subject of comparability. Of course, the reader will argue that culture and society are so different between Japan and the UK as to make nonsense of this argument. BUT, is this type of response an excuse for British failure? In their illuminating comparison of Japanese and American management, Pascale and Atlas leave us in no doubt on the issue:

> The dozen high-performing companies identified in our study of Japanese and American firms included six that were American. The prime determinant of their success was not society or culture; it was management.[3]

International markets are great levellers; British industry cannot opt out of being as effective in management as the Japanese and Americans. Remuneration forms part of that management exercise; it is not a prop for management nor a means to avoiding managing people, rather pay is part of a management strategy which embraces economic and social values in the mobilization of people contributions in the pursuit of corporate purpose.

References

1   Incomes Data Services Ltd. Study 260 February 1982
2   Incomes Data Services Ltd. Study 264 April 1982
3   PASCALE R T and ATHOS A G, *The art of Japanese management* Penguin Books 1982, p 205

Author index

Subject index